The Development of a Postmodern Self

Recent Titles in
Contributions in Sociology

The Development of a Postmodern Self

A COMPUTER-ASSISTED COMPARATIVE ANALYSIS OF PERSONAL DOCUMENTS

Michael R. Wood
AND
Louis A. Zurcher, Jr.

CONTRIBUTIONS IN SOCIOLOGY, NUMBER 70

Greenwood Press
New York • Westport, Connecticut • London

Library of Congress Cataloging-in-Publication Data

Wood, Michael R., 1949–
    The development of a postmodern self.

    (Contributions in sociology, ISSN 0084–9278 ;
no. 70)
    Bibliography: p.
    Includes index.
    1. American diaries—History and criticism.
2. American diaries—Data processing.   3. Self in
literature.   4. Postmodernism—United States.
I. Zurcher, Louis A.   II. Title.   III. Series.
PS409.W66   1988   303.4   87–23666
ISBN 0–313–25458–3 (lib. bdg. : alk. paper)

British Library Cataloguing in Publication Data is available.

Copyright © 1988 by Michael R. Wood and the Estate of Louis A. Zurcher, Jr.

All rights reserved. No portion of this book may be
reproduced, by any process or technique, without the
express written consent of the publisher.

Library of Congress Catalog Card Number: 87–23666
ISBN: 0–313–25458–3
ISSN: 0084–9278

First published in 1988

Greenwood Press, Inc.
88 Post Road West, Westport, Connecticut 06881

Printed in the United States of America

The paper used in this book complies with the
Permanent Paper Standard issued by the National
Information Standards Organization (Z39.48–1984).

10 9 8 7 6 5 4 3 2 1

Contents

Contents

Illustrations

FIGURES

The Development
of a Postmodern
Self

1

Introduction

The transformation of traditional and agrarian society brought about by the first Industrial Revolution was unprecedented and unparalleled. The term *industrial revolution* refers to the shift from an agrarian-based to an industrial-based economy that began with British precedent, spread to the continents of Europe and North America, and that continues in the present day. As the Western societies which had been the first to industrialize entered the latter part of the twentieth century various observers, social science and otherwise, began to forecast another "revolution" of momentous and far-reaching change. Some observers even compared the quality and pervasiveness of this change to the transformations wrought by industrial revolution, hence the terms *postindustrial revolution* and *postindustrial society*.

Arguments forecasting the emergence of postindustrial society have called attention to the birth of fundamentally new technologies (e.g., Wiener, 1954; Boulding, 1964; Toffler, 1980), the emergence of new classes of power holders (e.g., Galbraith, 1971; Bell, 1976), and especially to the expansion of service sector industries (e.g., Bell, 1976; Singelmann, 1978).

Arguments forecasting fundamental shifts in values, experience of self, and value orientations constitute a more diverse grouping, and do not necessarily include the designation *postindustrial* (e.g., Kavolis, 1970; Lifton, 1968; Yankelovich, 1981; Zurcher, 1977). A portion of these discussions is couched in terms of changes in individuals, personal values, attitudes, and conceptions of self. A portion draws attention to the emergence and generalization of subcultures sharing a rejection and critique of the established order. A third portion points to the change as a general phenomenon, with its wellsprings in the very heart of industrial society. These three perspectives will be labeled the "new self," the "new culture," and the "overdeveloped modernism" arguments.

Family resemblances justify referring to these perspectives collectively as *theories of a postmodern self* (cf. Kavolis, 1970). The family of postmodern self arguments forecasts/describes a shift in cultural conceptions of character and in definitions of self that is taking place in contemporary culture: from rationality and unemotional performance to irrationality, mysticism, and expressionism; from institutional standards, duty to society, achievement, and future time to individual standards, duty to self, gratification, and present time; and from structure, stability, and constancy to process, transience, multiplicity, and experimentation.

The study described in the following pages has a broad focus, and is concerned with the what, the how and when, and the why of the postmodern self. The first and most basic question is: What is the nature of the postmodern self? What are its dimensions? What are the form and content of the change in modern culture forecasted for the postmodern era? Second, how will the postmodern self develop, or how has it developed? When did it begin and what is the magnitude and rate of change? Third and finally, what are the reasons, the causes, and the explanations for the postmodern self? These questions call for both theoretical and empirical work: to determine limits and to impose structure on the ideas that collectively comprise the postmodern self theory, and to generate empirical data about its historical validity.

The empirical part of this book consists in an analysis of diaries from nineteenth- and twentieth-century American authors. Theoretical arguments describing the emergence of a postmodern self have typically been based on little if any systematic evidence. The present study attempts to address that shortfall by using one of the only sources of data available about the subjective experiences of individuals from both past and present time: personal documents, specifically, personal journals or diaries. In carrying out the analyses of diaries, both qualitative and quantitative techniques are employed. For the quantitative analysis, a computer approach is used in which the statistical incidence of particular words is examined over time.

Consequently, the purpose of the book is twofold: to advance theoretical and substantive knowledge about self and social change and to advance procedures for comparative analysis of personal documents. The volume is intended to be used by researchers, instructors, and advanced students interested in social psychology, social change, qualitative methods, and social science computer applications. For that reason the conceptual and methodological aspects of the study are described in detail.

The first five chapters formulate the theoretical question. Chapters 6 and 8 introduce the methodology of the study, including the computer-assisted technique used to analyze the personal documents. Chapters 7, 9, and 10 present the qualitative and quantitative findings regarding the postmodern self. Chapter 11 details a recasting of the theory.

2

The Background of the Postmodern Self: Industrial and Postindustrial Society

Postmodern self arguments presuppose the existence of a "modern" self and "modern" culture. Our discussion begins with consideration of the main structural and cultural features of industrial revolution, and the societies subsequently produced. We then consider arguments describing postindustrial society.

THE ECONOMIC AND SOCIAL BASE OF THE INDUSTRIAL REVOLUTION

The Industrial Revolution marks the span of the most significant transformation of human life recorded in written documents (Hobsbawm, 1969:13; 1962; Ashton, 1976; Cipolla, 1974; Hartwell, 1967; Heaton, 1967; Landes, 1969; Wrigley, 1969). Capitalized, the words *Industrial Revolution* denote the "first historical instance of the breakthrough from an agrarian, handicraft economy to one dominated by industry and machine manufacture" (Landes, 1969:1). The two most outstanding characteristics of the shift to an industrial economy are a sustained and qualitatively increased rate of economic growth, and a correspondingly revolutionary rate of population increase (Hartwell, 1967; Cipolla, 1974; Wrigley, 1969).

The Industrial Revolution began in Great Britain in the last third of the eighteenth century with a series of technological and manufacturing innovations in the production of cotton. Simple but effective technological innovations such as the "spinning jenny" of the 1760s, the "water frame" of 1768, and the "mule" of the 1780s adjusted the labor imbalance between spinning and weaving by making it possible (using the sources of inanimate energy that were becoming available) for spinners to keep yarn supplies abreast of the demands of weavers for the first time. The mechanization of weaving did not take place on any widespread scale until after the turn of the century, though, as with the case of spinning, the technology involved was either pre-existing (a power loom had been invented in the 1780s) or relatively simple (Hobsbawm, 1969:58–59; Ashton, 1976; Deane, 1965; Landes, 1969).[1]

Conjunctive with these technological improvements, the factory system of production was introduced, with its division of labor, routinization of work, and rhythm of the machine. To many contemporaries, the new order of the day (which they saw exemplified in Lancashire) seemed to consist of three elements: (1) the formation of a class of propertyless wage laborers who confronted capitalist owners and employers; (2) the factory system itself, or organization of production within specialized structures where specialized tasks were performed through the use of machines utilizing inanimate power; and (3) the domination of the whole life of society by the restless pursuit of profit by the capitalists (Hobsbawm, 1969:66–67; Marx, 1967; Engels, 1958). From a twentieth-century perspective such views seem inaccurate, but not unreasonable. The cotton factory system hardly affected a majority of the labor force, was technologically far behind the railway which followed only shortly, and possessed a decentralized and generally archaic business structure. Yet the fact that the cotton mills did inspire such visions of dehumanization and narrowing of work, of working people transformed into "hands" or "operatives" eventually to be replaced completely by fully automatic machinery, is significant.[2] As Hobsbawm (1969:68) observed: "The 'factory' with its logical flow of processes, each a specialized machine tended by a specialized 'hand,' all linked together by the inhuman and constant pace of the 'engine' and the discipline of mechanization, gas-lit, iron-ribbed and smoking, *was* a revolutionary form of work" (see also Landes, 1969:43).

The second phase of industrialization (ca. 1840–1895) had its inception as the textile manufacturing industry began to decline, and was based on the more economically sound capital goods industries—on coal, iron, and steel. Part of the reason for the emergence of the capital goods–based second phase of industrialization was the expanding world market of countries now beginning to industrialize and consequently needing metals and machinery. Along with this was a factor having little to do with the growth of demand, namely, the pressure of accumulated British capital for investment. The emerging accumulation of capital and the income accrued from the products of the "workshop of the world" ushered in the second phase of the Industrial Revolution, the great age of railway construction.

The railroad received an abundance of capital built up by previous industrialization, and railways were built at a feverish pace, especially during the "railway manias" of 1835–1837 and 1845–1847. As a result of the pell-mell pace of construction the British railway system was more or less complete by 1850 (Hobsbawm, 1969:109–113; Deane, 1965). The railway represented a technologically far more advanced phase of industrialization, and affected a much larger segment of the population than the relatively small number of persons who lived in the immediate vicinity of actual industry. The building of railroads, and the subsequent nationwide interlocking transportation net with its accompanying systematized timetable, impressed the populace at large of the revolutionary nature of the new age even more than the industrialization of cotton (Hobsbawm, 1969).

France, Germany, and the United States developed later than the British pioneer, and their industrialization was to an extent unique in each country. Nevertheless the revolutionary impact of industrialization was the same: in each case a radical change occurred not only in the methods and level of output of economic production, but in transportation, communication, population, and in social and cultural organization as well.[3] Henry Adams, an American born in 1838, looked back on his childhood years as a historic turning point of significance exceeding any that "had ever happened before in human experience," a time in which "the old universe was thrown into the ash heap and a new one created" (quoted in Miller, 1970:ix). Adams was singularly impressed by events of 1844 which seemed to him to signal the final dissolution of one era and the birth of a new one—"by the opening of the Boston and Albany railroad; the appearance of the first Cunard steamers in the bay; and the telegraphic messages which carried from Baltimore to Washington the news that Henry Clay and James K. Polk were nominated for the Presidency" (Adams, quoted in Miller, 1970:ix).

Demographic explosion, in addition to sustained economic growth, is the other major structural feature of industrial revolution. The agricultural revolution (ca. 7000–5000 BC) significantly increased the supply of disposable animal and plant energy available to human societies, resulting in an increase in the rate of population growth and in the total number of persons that the land could support (Cipolla, 1974; Wrigley, 1969). Industrialization, however, produced increases in both energy and population far in excess of what had gone before. The population of England and Wales, for example, which remained virtually unchanged during the early decades of the eighteenth century, expanded at a rate of about 7 percent in the 1750s, to over 10 percent in the 1790s, to a peak of about 16 percent in the second decade of the nineteenth century (Deane, 1965:32; Wrigley, 1969).

Urban areas grew in conjunction with the expanding population. The new industrial city of Manchester, which shocked many foreign visitors in the 1830s and 1840s, swelled tenfold in size between 1760 and 1830— from 17,000 to 180,000 persons (Hobsbawm, 1969:56).[4] During the two decades between 1820 and 1840, Philadelphia and its surrounding area increased from 100,000 to over 200,000; and America's largest metropolis, New York, multiplied from 123,000 to over 321,000 (Miller, 1970:39). Less than one-fifth of the U.S. population lived in towns of 2,500 people or more prior to the Civil War, but by the beginning of the twentieth century 40 percent of the American populace were urban dwellers (Degler, 1977:43; Weisberger, 1969).

CULTURE, KNOWLEDGE, AND INDUSTRIAL REVOLUTION

The economic and social structural changes that made up the Industrial Revolution occurred integrally with developments in knowledge, ideas, and ways of thinking. The culture of modern industrial society that had emerged by the end of the nineteenth century has been described by economic historians and sociologists as having as one of its keynote themes the rationality of *means* adapted to *ends*—particularly, the "ends" of profit and accumulation of capital, and the "means" of production organized on the basis of machinery, inanimate power, and division of labor (the factory system).

Practical rationality characterized the early phase of industrialization. The revolutionary element was not so much technical invention as the rational and practical application of technology in view of opportunities promised by expanding markets.

The technology of cotton manufacture was thus fairly simple, and so, as we shall see, was that of most of the rest of the changes which collectively made up the "Industrial Revolution." It required little scientific knowledge or technical skill beyond the scope of a practical mechanic of the early eighteenth century.
. . .
The early Industrial Revolution was technically rather primitive not because no better science and technology was available, or because men took no interest in it or could not be persuaded to use it. It was simple because, by and large, the application of simple ideas and devices, often of ideas available for centuries, often by no means expensive, could produce striking results. The novelty lay not in the innovations, but in the readiness of practical men to put their minds to using the science and technology which had long been available and within reach; and in the wide market which lay open to goods as prices and costs fell rapidly (Hobsbawm, 1969:59–60).

Landes (1969) reached conclusions similar to Hobsbawm's from his study of technological change and industrial development in Western Europe from 1750 to the modern era. Landes isolated rationality ("adaptation of means to ends") and its logical corollary, continuous adaptation and change, as the essential principle of industrial revolution.

When all the complicating circumstances are stripped away—changing technology, shifting ratios of factor costs, diverse market structures in diverse economic and political systems—two things remain and characterize any modern industrial system: rationality, which is the spirit of the institution, and change, which is rationality's logical corollary, for the appropriation of means to ends that is the essence of rationality implies a process of continuous adaptation (Landes, 1969:546).

Historical characterizations of the culture and knowledge of the Industrial Revolution given by Hobsbawm, Landes, and other economic historians are complemented and reinforced by Weber's (1927; 1946; 1958; 1968; 1978a; 1978b) more comprehensive analysis. Weber's investigation of the Industrial Revolution was conducted in the context of his interests in Western, and indeed, world, social, and cultural development.

Means-ends rationality, the distinguishing characteristic of the Industrial Revolution identified by Hobsbawm and Landes, was recognized by Weber. However, Weber saw "rationality" as a focal concept of central importance for a sociological analysis of modern society. Weber's remarks on the culture of the Industrial Revolution occur in the context of his extensive and comprehensive analysis of modern "rationalized" capitalism.[5]

The provision of the needs of a human group by the method of private enterprise seeking profit is what is meant by "capitalism," and in this sense capitalism appeared historically as early as ancient Babylon (Weber, 1927; Collins, 1980). What is distinctive about the modern form of capitalism that emerged apace with industrial revolution was its comprehensive application of *rational calculation* to all aspects of the economic function, and indeed, to other institutional spheres of society as well. "The key term is *calculability*. . . . What is distinctive about modern, large-scale, rational capitalism—in contrast to earlier, partial forms—is that it is methodical and predictable, reducing all areas of production and distribution as much as possible to a routine" (Collins, 1980:927).

Weber's analysis of the Industrial Revolution puts emphasis not on technological breakthrough but on the infrastructure and institutional context which stimulated technological innovation. The attitude of calculating rationality called for innovation in the productive process as a means of lowering costs, in view of a projection of corresponding increments of profit.

Rational calculation was embodied not only in the economic sector but in other institutional sectors of society as well, especially law and

administration. In addition to rational calculation in the production process itself—workplace, tools and machinery, sources of power, and labor—rational calculation characterized the legal and administrative
environment. Modern capitalism presupposes a calculable legal and administrative environment. "The modern capitalist enterprise rests primarily on *calculation* and presupposes a legal and administrative system,
whose functioning can be rationally predicted, at least in principle, by
virtue of its fixed general norms, just like the expected performance of
a machine" (Weber, 1978a:1394).

The rationality of calculation that Weber saw as an elemental and
singularly pervasive feature of Western industrial society may be termed
formal rationality. Formal rationality occurs in its purest state in the rationality of economic action, where it means the extent of quantitative
calculation applied to an economic action (Weber, 1978a:85). A more
general interpretation of formal rationality, in which it is seen as a master
theme for analysis of capitalist industrial society, defines it in terms of
the *calculability of means and procedures* (Brubaker, 1984:36). "From the
point of view of the purely formal objective of maximizing the calculability of action —purely formal because maximally calculable action can
be oriented to any of an infinite variety of possible substantive ends—
capitalism, science, technology, and the modern legal and administrative
system are highly rational" (Brubaker, 1984:36).

It is important to Weber's sociological analysis of Western industrial
society as well as for our theoretical interpretation of the postmodern
self to underline the fact that the imposing presence of formal rationality
existed in tension with a deficit of *substantive rationality*, that is, "rationality from the point of view of some particular substantive end, belief,
or value commitment" (Brubaker, 1984:36). Capitalist industrial society
embodied formal rationality but for this very reason lacked substantive
rationality.

Substantive rationality (to return to the economic sphere) means the
extent to which the outcome of an economic process corresponds to
some criterion of ultimate values. While formal rationality is a matter of
fact, substantive rationality is a matter of value. Substantive rationality
refers primarily to the *"value* (from some explicitly defined standpoint)
of ends or results" (Brubaker, 1984:36). To call a procedure formally rational is to say it is based on goal-oriented rational calculation and em-
ploys the most technically adequate available methods; to say an action
or procedure is substantively rational, however, is to apply "criteria of
ultimate ends, whether they be ethical, political, utilitarian, hedonistic,
feudal, egalitarian, or whatever, and measure the results of the economic
action" (Weber, 1978a:85).

The tension between formal and substantive rationality is a major
theme of Weber's sociological analysis of modern society and will pro-

vide a point of departure for our later recasting of postmodern self theory in light of the results of the study.

Contemporary Observations

The observations of contemporary sociologists and social psychologists studying the continuing process of economic development and modernization are consistent with the ideas of Weber and the economic historians. Illustrative of these is the work of Inkeles and colleagues (Inkeles, 1973; Inkeles and Smith, 1974; Inkeles, 1983). Summarizing the results of a study of 6,000 men from six developing countries, Inkeles (1973:342–343) noted: "To a striking degree, the same syndrome of attitudes, values and ways of acting . . . defines the modern man in each of the six countries and in all the occupational groups of cultivator, craftsman, and industrial worker." The shared characteristics of individual modernity included openness to innovation and change, independence from traditional beliefs and authority figures, a rejection of magic and a corresponding belief in science, a sense of efficacy, and a belief in planning and calculability.

Berger et al. (1973) described the content and structure of consciousness characteristic of "modernity" from the perspective of the sociology of knowledge. Some of the elements of the modern cognitive style they described were: its comprehension of reality as composed of separate and interchangeable components; separability of means and ends; conception and understanding of animate and inanimate action in an abstract frame of reference; segregation of knowledge of work world from family and other worlds; problem-solving inventiveness and a tinkering attitude; anonymous social relations and anonymous experience of self ("self-anonymization"); emotional management and control; assumption of maximalization ("bigger and better"); and ability to relate to many levels of reality at once (Berger et al., 1973).

THE EMERGENCE OF POSTINDUSTRIAL SOCIETY

A major feature of industrialization, as mentioned in Chapter 1, is the retreat of the agricultural sector of the economy in the face of advance by industry and factory manufacture, so that the latter become the predominant productive sectors. The movement of workers from agriculture to industry, transportation, and trade is a major feature of industrialization. By 1890, for example, 57 percent of the U.S. labor force worked outside of agriculture, while farmers and farm workers had composed over half of the population of workers only twenty years earlier. During the 1880s, the number of industrial workers grew 50 percent, capital invested jumped 137 percent and by 1890, the annual value of manufactured goods exceeded that of agricultural commodities for the first time in American history (Degler, 1977:3). During the twentieth century the decrease in the proportion of labor employed by agriculture that is part and parcel of the industrialization process continued. The trend progressed to an extent probably exceeding what most nineteenth-century observers would have thought possible, so that by 1970 U.S. employment in agriculture had declined to less than 4 percent of the total labor force (Singelmann, 1978; Stanback et al , 1981).

In addition to an unprecedented decrease of the agricultural work force, a dramatic increase in the proportion of labor employed by the tertiary or service sector has occurred in the latter twentieth century. By 1972 the service sector employed 50 percent or more of the total work force in at least six industrialized countries, and in the United States currently accounts for nearly seven out of every ten jobs (Sorrentino, 1971; Stanback et al., 1981). Considering trends in the United States for the one-hundred-year period between 1870 and 1970, the proportion of the labor force employed by the "extractive" sector (including agriculture, fishing, forestry, and mining) declined spectacularly, from 52 percent to about 4 percent (Browning and Singelmann, 1975; Singelmann, 1978). The "transformative" sector (including construction and manufacturing) increased its proportionate share of the labor force from roughly one-quarter to one-third. But the service sector experienced the greatest gains in labor expansion during this period: "distributive" services (including transportation, trade, and communication) rose from 11.5 to 22.3 percent; "producer" services (including banking, insurance, accounting, and legal) increased from 2.8 to 8.2 percent (1920 to 1970); "social" services (including education, health, and government) swelled from 8.7 to 21.9 percent (1920 to 1970); and finally, "personal" services (including domestic, hotel, eating and drinking, repair, and entertainment) rose from 8.2 to 10.0 percent (1920 to 1970) (Browning and Singelmann, 1975:9–12; see also Stanback et al., 1981:10–21).

Proponents of the "postindustrial revolution" thesis have stressed that important consequences will follow from the emergence of the service sector as the major employer of the work force. These include significant changes in work activities and attitudes, and importantly, in social relations. According to Bell (1976:127):

A post-industrial society is based on services. Hence, it is a game between persons. What counts is not raw muscle power, or energy, but information. The central person is the professional, for he is equipped, by his education and training, to provide the kinds of skill which are increasingly demanded in the post-industrial society. If an industrial society is defined by the quantity of goods as marking a standard of living, the post-industrial society is defined by the quality of life as measured by the services and amenities—health, education, recreation, and the arts—which are now deemed desirable and possible for everyone.

Fuchs (1968:189) observed that the growth of service industries would entail a lessening of work alienation and an increase in opportunities for creative work.

Employees in many services are closely related to their work and often render a highly personalized service that offers ample scope for the development and excercise of personal skills.

This is true of some goods-producing occupations as well, but the direct confrontation between consumer and worker that occurs frequently in services creates the possibility of a more completely human and satisfying work experience. . . . With more and more people becoming engaged in service occupations, the net effect for the labor force as a whole may be in the direction of the *personalization* of work.

A second major component of the postindustrial revolution thesis is the perception of the emergence of a "new" technology. One of the first discussions of the new technology was Wiener's (1954) announcement of a "Second Industrial Revolution" associated with the development of the computer and various sophisticated communications systems and inventions in electronics. After Wiener, other observers announced the emergence of a new technology as different from industrial technology as industrial technology was from its counterpart in agrarian society. These included, for example, Kahn and A. J. Wiener (1967a; 1967b), Brzezinski (1970), Boulding (1964), Toffler (1970; 1980), and Williams (1982). These arguments generally called attention to the distinguishing factors of the postindustrial revolution in technology as "the emergence of computer technology, rapid development in electronics, communications, and behavior control, and widespread use of 'intellectual' or 'software' technologies, such as operations research, linear programming, and systems design" (Gendron, 1977:19).

A third major component of the postindustrial revolution thesis is the idea that the new technology will entail significant changes in the decision-making structure of the economy, and eventually in the larger society: technical experts will replace capitalists as the new captains of industry. An important consequence of this change will be a shift in goals from profit and competition to planning, rational control of the economy, and quality of life.

Bell (1976) and Galbraith (1971) argued for the political and economic significance of the emergence of the class of technocrats and knowledge producers. Bell observed that the dominant figures in postindustrial society would not be entrepreneurs, businessmen, or industrial executives, but scientists, mathematicians, economists, and engineers of the

new intellectual technology. About decision making Bell (1976:344)
noted:

> In the post-industrial society, production and business decisions will be sub-
> ordinated to, or will derive from, other forces in society; the crucial decisions
> regarding the growth of the economy and its balance will come from government,
> but they will be based on the government's sponsorship of research and de-
> velopment, of cost-effectiveness and cost-benefit analysis; the making of deci-
> sions, because of the intricately linked nature of their consequences, will have
> an increasingly technical character.

Galbraith argued that planning would become a necessity in the new
industrial state, due mainly to the demands of postindustrial technology.
The market would be superseded as a regulator of production and replaced by the planning of technological elites—the technostructure.

> In the industrial enterprise, power rests with those who make decisions. In
> the mature enterprise, this power has passed, inevitably and irrevocably, from
> the individual to the group. That is because only the group has the information
> that decision requires. Though the constitution of the corporation places power
> in the hands of the owners, the imperatives of technology and planning remove
> it to the technostructure (Galbraith, 1971:109).

The goals of the technostructure included a secure level of earnings
and a maximal rate of growth, and to a lesser extent, technological
virtuosity and a rising dividend rate. But unlike the old power structure,
the technostructure was at least willing to consider the implementation
of social and community goals provided that its primary goals of adequate growth and earnings were achieved.

While it does not fall within the scope of this book to examine critically
postindustrial revolution predictions about economic change, we will
make reference to some of the major criticisms. On the matter of the
new technology, the question has been asked why the introduction of
computer, communications, behavioral, and managerial technologies
should count as part of a major revolution in technology while the
internal combustion engine and the development of nuclear power and
weapons are considered as only as important developments within an
already existing industrial technology (Gendron, 1977). Second, it has
been objected that instead of a situation in which the "knowledgeable
have power," postindustrial society may turn out to be rather a setting
in which the "powerful have knowledge"—the old corporate structure
may learn to control the technocrats and prevent a power transfer (Giddens, 1973). Finally, it has been objected that the plain fact of the changed
composition of the labor force does not necessarily imply a real change
either in the character of work as experienced by the typical service

worker, or in long-standing demands by workers such as the call for more control over the work situation (Birnbaum, 1971; Braverman, 1974; Hochschild, 1983).

NOTES

1. On the technological simplicity of the power loom see Edmund Cartwright's autobiographical account of his invention, reproduced in part in Clough and Moodie (1965).

2. But see Kasson (1976) for an account of the embracing of the new technology by the young American republic.

3. For an account of some of the more neglected scientific developments of the nineteenth century that had a significant impact on industry, see Bernal (1969).

4. Visitors such as Frederick Engels (1958) and Alexis de Tocqueville (Kasson, 1976:56–57).

5. The complexities and ambiguities of Weber's writings are well known. The following account relies on expository and systematizing efforts (Kalberg, 1980; Collins, 1980; Schluchter, 1981; Brubaker, 1984), as well as on translated texts.

3

Speculations on a "New Self"

Having outlined changes in social and economic organization pointed to by depictions of postindustrial society, our task now is to discuss predictions about change in culture and the experience of self which are also forecasted for roughly the same era (i.e., late twentieth century). Discussions and speculations on these changes will be analytically divided into "new self" and "new culture" arguments which emphasize the novel and emergent character of these changes, and "overdeveloped modernism" arguments which emphasize the continuity of change. The term *postmodern self* is used here to refer collectively to all three.

Speculations on a new self point to the emergence in the United States of a new experience of self and identity, a shift in values and conceptions of character. New self arguments usually, but not always, identify social structural characteristics that are associated with the postindustrial revolution argument. Identity and self-concept themes described as increasing and becoming more extensive include: irrationality, mysticism, and expression over rationality and unemotional performance (Kavolis, 1970; Adler, 1968); individual standards, spontaneity, discovery, and present time, versus institutional standards, duty to society, achievement, and future time (Turner, 1976); multiplicity, experimentation, transience, change, and process (Zurcher, 1977; Simmel, 1971; Lifton, 1968).

A similar group of ideas is contained in arguments which are framed in terms of broad shifts in culture and values rather than definitions of self. There are two accounts of a new culture in postindustrial society. Historically prior are *counterculture* arguments. This term will be used to refer to the observations of those who see the emerging new culture as part of a critique and reaction to capitalist industrial society. Closer to the present, and framed in terms of thesis rather than antithesis, the "new rules" argument updates and describes the generalizations of counterculture arguments.

The counterculture is concerned with the non-intellectual and with inner experience over the rational and objective, with the magical, the mystic, the occult, and psychic (Roszak, 1969). It accepts the self and not society as the true reality, and it accepts only the duty to actualize one's self as the true duty of life—not duty imposed by society (Reich, 1970). It also rejects delayed gratification and restraint and chooses stimulation, openness to experience, and expressiveness (Slater, 1970).

Subsequent to the heyday of the counterculture (late 1960s, early 1970s) many of its themes became generalized and merged with other cultural currents. The "new rules" for living which were known to a majority of Americans by the 1980s stressed especially the duty of individuals to themselves and their happiness and enjoyment, rather than to institutions and social roles (Yankelovich, 1981).

A third variation on the postmodern self theme is comprised by the observations of social and cultural analysts who take a more comprehensive view of the phenomenon. The basic argument of "overdeveloped modernism" is that the emergence of postmodern self is part of a larger and more general phenomenon, the continued cultural development of industrial society. From this perspective the change is viewed as emerging out of, and as representing continuity with modern industrial society and culture. The emerging postmodern self is seen as both consonant and discordant with its origins, the "overripe" (to use Sorokin's metaphor) yield of the process of cultural modernization that began with the advent of industrialization and the emergence of capitalism.

The character of modern culture viewed from this standpoint is one of becoming, change, process, transformation, flux, formlessness, uncertainty, sensual gratification, and a focus on the present (Sorokin, 1957); a desire for individuation, for new forms of experience, for self-enhancement and self-actualization, and a new appreciation of the values of hedonism (Bell, 1976).

INSTITUTION-IMPULSE/PRODUCT-PROCESS

Before discussing the new self, new culture, and overdeveloped modernism arguments in more detail, the conceptual framework that guided the research effort will be elaborated. It will be argued that there are two related yet analytically distinct dimensions or meaning clusters among the postmodern self discussions (see Schneider, 1971).

The first meaning cluster is marked by a contrast between the restraining, institutional, and moral component of personality and the unrestrained, instinctual, and biological component. Although Freud is usually not cited explicitly, it is probably no accident that a concern with these themes is shown by particular authors. This cluster of meanings will be termed *Institution-Impulse* (Turner, 1976), where *Institution* refers to the themes of authority and conformity, rationality, law and duty. The opposing category, *Impulse*, refers to themes of emotion, experience, irrationality, and nonconformity.

The second cluster deals more directly with the personal experience of self and conception of identity. This meaning cluster will be called *Product-Process*. The self can be viewed as an outcome, an object to be attained or somehow accomplished; alternatively, it can be viewed as an activity or process that has no definite goal other than its own continued development and actualization of potential. The distinction made is between self as Product and self as Process, and corresponds to the process-product ambiguity of words such as *education, deduction,* and *science* (Rudner, 1966). *Product* will refer to themes of form and structure, constancy and duration, finishing and outcomes, completion, achievement, attainment and future time. *Process,* the opposing category, will refer to themes of multiplicity, movement and succession, alteration and transience, discovery, spontaneity, and present time.

The Institution-Impulse meaning cluster probably needs no additional elaboration here, but the reader may wish for more clarification of the Product-Process cluster. An example of the Product type of self-conception would be the religious person who is trying to achieve salvation through a faultless adherence to a prescribed mode of conduct, or the business manager who aspires above all else to become company president and who thinks not of a life in the present but only of the future when the goal is attained. For this kind of identity the self is oriented primarily in reference to a goal (or combination of goals), the goal state itself being an endpoint from which no further development is deemed necessary or even possible.

By contrast, the Process self does not aspire to a goal from which further change would be superfluous, but instead is oriented toward growth, toward a continuous "becoming." The religious believer who strives for continued spiritual development and sacred experience each day and the executive who changes positions in search of fulfillment of personal potential would both be examples of Process type identities.

Taken together, the two meaning clusters of Institution-Impulse and Product-Process make a distinction between the structure of self and identity, and its working or functioning. A similar distinction was made by Parsons and colleagues (Parsons et al., 1951; see Holsti, 1969) between complexes of qualities and complexes of performance in the composition of social objects, where complexes of qualities referred to what an object was, and complexes of performance referred to what it did.

THE NEW SELF

Variants of the postmodern self argument framed in terms of changes in individual self-concept include discussions where the focus is more on Institution-Impulse, or more on Product-Process. Discussions focusing more on Institution-Impulse will be considered first, including works by Adler, Kavolis, and Turner. Discussions that focus more on Product-Process include works by Lifton, Simmel, and Zurcher.

Institution vs. Impulse

Adler described a "personality type" which he believed to be increasing in contemporary society. He called this personality type the *antinomian*, a term typically appearing in theological vocabulary. "Antinomianism designated those values and behaviors that challenged ecclesiastical authority and questioned moral law—hence its appropriateness for current unconventional behavior" (Adler, 1968:326; 1972). Adler's thesis was that the antinomian character type was not new but had occurred many times in the past; it was a kind of personality that would be found at any historical time period during conditions of social instability.

Adler viewed the antinomian personality as a pathological coping response to decay of, or threats to, an individual's frame of reference. His explanation of the antinomian personality was based on his view that stability and order are necessary for normal human functioning. "In a stable, orderly world what is construed as 'human nature' appears self-evident and lawful. Parts seem related to the whole. Morale is high and an optimistic, naturalistic, and rational orientation is dominant" (Adler, 1968:330). The recognition of order constituted "the armature on which the self and its identity are built" (Adler, 1968:330). When this armature collapsed during times of social instability and crisis, "A new scaffold for the self becomes necessary; other manipulations of sensory and perceptual inputs are required to stabilize and master the threatened self" (Adler, 1968:330).

The antinomian orientation was an attempt to re-establish order in the self in the face of instability and crisis. The antinomian switched allegiance from a decaying institutional order—from the abstract, the generalized, and the cognitive, to the physical, the visceral, and the concrete. Feeling, texture, touch, and warmth became more important than central modes of cognitive functioning. "The antinomian personality values most the immediate and the vivid, the uninhibited and the outrageous" (Adler, 1968:327).

The antinomian shifted to a present time perspective and made a "cult of immediacy." This shift to "now or never" helped the antinomian "to anchor a self which repudiates control, tolerates no delay, and typically challenges the 'Establishment,' whose conventions and authority" were denied (Adler, 1968:330). In a statement reminiscent of psychoanalytic terminology Adler stated (1968:330) that the antinomian "asserts the primacy of the 'natural self' and of its impulses and desires, rejecting counsels of discrimination and control."

Adler viewed the personality configuration and values identified with the 1960s hippie movement as merely the present manifestation of the antinomian type that had appeared in many different forms. Past manifestations included the Gnostics and other religious heretics, and the romantic movement in art.

Kavolis (1970) identified a complex of values, traits, and orientations similar to Adler's antinomian type, which he called the "underground" personality. The underground self was a self based on the Impulse themes of irrationality, expressiveness, and emotion. The underground self had gone largely unnoticed possibly because of preoccupation with the secular-rationalistic "modern" personality which had been propounded in theories of psychological modernization. Kavolis (1970:436) believed that both "modern" and "underground" types were emerging in the modern world, largely as a counterpart of sociocultural change "toward an increasingly rationalized bureaucracy. . . ." The "psychological resultant" of such trends might be "a more rationally organized and unemotionally performing type of personality, concerned only with the orderly application of rules rather than with the solution of immediate existential or ultimate metaphysical problems" (Kavolis, 1970:436; see also Merton, 1968:251–254). But, as a reaction to such trends, "an exaggeratedly irrational kind of personality might emerge—one inclined toward anarchic romanticism, expressionism, mysticism, and the politics and education of ecstasy" (Kavolis, 1970:436). Thus, "psychological modernization" appeared to be a process of increasing tension between these two alternatives.

According to Kavolis (1970:445) the underground personality rejected restraints, had a need to reassert individual and group uniqueness, and valued sensuous experience of concrete details. There was also an insistence on immediate satisfaction, and an orientation to bodily sensations and feelings. Those values and preferences were by and large the opposite of those associated with the rationally organized modern personality.

Kavolis also described a third type, the "postmodern," a personality "characterized by the sense that both polarities of a great many of these dilemmas are contained, in an unresolved form, within one's own ex-perience" (1970:445). That is, both the "modernistic" and "under-ground" elements were recognized as components of the self by this type of personality. Kavolis did not describe the "postmodern" type in any detail, and it would appear that he viewed it more as a possibility than as an actual occurrence.

Turner (1976:989; Turner and Schutte, 1981) described two modes or loci of self-realization that he called "institution" and "impulse." "It is proposed that people variously recognize their real selves either in feel-ings and actions of an institutional and volitional nature, such as am-bition, morality, and altruism, or in the experience of impulse, such as undisciplined desire and the wish to make intimate revelations to other people." Turner believed that in "recent decades" a shift in the locus of self had occurred, from an institutional locus to an impulse locus.

Turner (1976:992–995) listed several crucial differences between the contrasting poles of self-realization:

1. For institutionals the self is revealed through adherence to a high standard, especially in spite of adverse conditions. Impulsives value instead action for its own sake; the self is revealed when action is undertaken wholly as a result of personal choice.

2. From the institutional perspective the self is something to be created or achieved, it is an outcome. Impulsives search for the self in the present, it must be discovered.

3. Institutionals realize the self in the control and regulation of action, valuing inhibition and sublimation. Impulsives see the true self revealed only when inhibitions are lifted and behavior is spontaneous.

4. Hypocrisy is negatively valued by both types, but two different kinds of hypocrisy are at issue. The institutional seeks congruence between "prescrip-tion and behavior"; failing to live up to one's standards is held in disregard. Impulsives seek congruence between "impulse and behavior." They define a hypocrite as anyone who lives according to standards that do not correspond to his/her personal likes and dislikes.

5. A polished, error-free performance in which the actor's personality is sub-merged is admired by institutionals. Imperfections, evidence of the actor's human frailties, indicate a successful performance from the impulse point of view.

6. As suggested by the difference between discovery and achievement, impul-sives view the self from a present time perspective. Institutionals are oriented toward the future and suffer self-estrangement when a future perspective is threatened or felt to be unfeasible.

7. Social or peer pressure that diverts a person from achievement or adherence to ethical standards is rejected by institutionals. Impulsives, on the other hand, reject institutional and societal pressures that force persons into courses of action contrary to their natural wishes and impulses.

Although Turner identified the shift from institution to impulse as occurring in recent decades he nevertheless cited nineteenth-century authors such as Wordsworth and Blake for illustrations of the impulse perspective—as did Adler in describing the antinomian. Turner advised that the shift should be examined in light of a larger historical context, and that the factors of rural-urban differences, class differences, cultural differences, and dissimilarities between generations should not be overlooked.

Product vs. Process

Many of Turner's statements about the emerging impulse fit into the Product-Process meaning cluster, especially the discussion of achievement versus discovery, and future orientation versus present time focus.

Postmodern self discussions dealing more with Product-Process will now be considered, including works by Lifton, Simmel, and Zurcher.

Lifton (1968:13; 1969) described a "set of psychological patterns characteristic of contemporary life" that were creating a new kind of person, the "protean." To lay double stress upon the themes of change and flux, the terms *character* and *personality* (suggesting fixity and permanence) were avoided in favor of the term *self-process* to describe the Protean Self.

Lifton believed that the new style of self-process was emerging largely as a result of the disproportionate influence of one of three general factors which shape human behavior. The three factors were "the psychobiological potential common to all mankind at any moment in time; those traits given special emphasis in a particular cultural tradition; and those related to modern (and particularly contemporary) historical forces" (Lifton, 1968:13).

Lifton's thesis was that two main features of modern historical forces were the principal shapers of the protean self-process (1968:16). These were (1) historical (or psychohistorical) dislocation, "the break in the sense of connection which men have long felt with the vital and nourishing symbols of their cultural tradition"; and (2) flooding of imagery "produced by the extraordinary flow of postmodern cultural influences over mass communication networks."

Descriptions of the protean self-process given by Lifton emphasized multiplicity, transience, and alteration. "The protean style of self-process, then, is characterized by an interminable series of experiments— some shallow, some profound—each of which may be readily abandoned in favor of still new psychological quests" (Lifton, 1968:17). The Protean Self resembled what Erikson (1963) called "identity diffusion." However, the protean style was not pathological, and could possibly be one of the adaptive patterns of contemporary times.

Lifton's ideas about the emerging protean were based on his observations in America, Europe, and Japan, drawn from patients in psy-
chotherapy as well as literary and artistic figures. He quoted the
comments of a young teacher to illustrate the protean pattern (1968:17):

I have an extraordinary number of masks I can put on or take off. The question
is: is there, or should there be, one face which should be authentic? I'm not
sure that there is one for me. I can think of other parallels to this, especially in
literature. There are representations of every kind of crime, every kind of sin.
For me, there is not a single act I cannot imagine myself committing.

Lifton gave other illustrations from such diverse sources as Jean-Paul
Sartre and Marcello Mastroianni. All emphasized the lack of structure,
the lack of permanence, and the great capacity for change of the protean
self-process. Additional themes characterizing the protean were a sense
of absurdity expressed as mockery, suspicion of nurturance as a threat
to autonomy, and hidden guilt caused by a sense of having no suitable
objects of loyalty and commitment.

Overreaching all of these areas was "a profound psychic struggle with
the idea of change itself" (Lifton, 1968:25). The Protean Self was attracted
to the idea of continuous transformation and at the same time repelled
by it, once again exhibiting characteristic ambivalence. A glorious future
of incessant transmutation was alternately viewed by the protean as a
frightening transmogrification, and a golden age of absolute oneness in
the past was longed for. But whatever the course of action taken by the
protean, he "carried with him an extraordinary range of possiblility for
man's betterment, or more important, for his survival" (Lifton, 1968:27).

Simmel's (1971) essays about the experience of modern life contained
both Institution-Impulse and Product-Process themes, but Simmel seems
to have placed more emphasis on the processual and protean character
of modern self-consciousness. Simmel is unique among the "new self"
authors because his observations date from the turn of the nineteenth
into the twentieth century.

Simmel's descriptions of the form of modern individuality stressed
the themes of experimentation, change, and process. He cited nineteenth-century romanticism as perhaps the most important vehicle of
the dissemination of the modern style of individualism. In terms strik-
ingly similar to later authors, he described the romantic psyche (1971:224)
as "an endless succession of contrasts," a "protean succession of contrasting moods and tasks, beliefs and feelings."

Similar themes were emphasized in Simmel's discussion of the modern
versus the Greek experience of life (1971:238). "The *dynamic* vital character of the modern life-feeling, and the fact that it is manifest to us as
a form of vital *movement*, consumed in a continuous flux in spite of all

persistence and faithfulness, and adhering to a rhythm that is always new—this runs counter to the Greek's sense of substance and its eternal outline."

Simmel achieved a more comprehensive and systematic theoretical synthesis of these themes in his essay "The Conflict in Modern Culture." Life, as he viewed it, was a continuous process but a process that could become manifest only in the production of particular forms. Once produced, however, forms necessarily had to clash with life since life was in ceaseless flux. Thus, owing to the "essential restlessness" of life, it "constantly struggles against its own products, which have become fixed and do not move along with it" (Simmel, 1971:376).

The conflict between the process of life and its products manifests itself as a continuous displacement and usurpment of old forms by new ones. The distinctive feature of modern life rendering it so different from the past was that now life seemed to be struggling against the very principle of form. "At present, we are experiencing a new phase of the old struggle—no longer a struggle of a contemporary form, filled with life, against an old, lifeless one, but a struggle of life against the form *as such*, against the *principle* of form" (Simmel, 1971:377).

Life's struggle with its products reached a new intensity in the modern world, and an era altogether lacking in forms seemed to be commencing. "The bridge between the past and the future of cultural forms seems to be demolished; we gaze into an abyss of unformed life beneath our feet. But perhaps this formlessness is itself the appropriate form for contemporary life" (Simmel, 1971:393).

Simmel illustrated his ideas about the modern revolt against form by citing cultural trends and developments in philosophy (e.g., Schopenhauer and Nietzsche), art (e.g., expressionism), and ethics and religion ("the new morality" and mysticism). He noted that historical changes of a revolutionary impact have usually been borne by youth, a fact especially true of the contemporary revolt against forms.

The desire for completely abstract art among some sectors of modern youth may stem from passion for an immediate and unrestrained [*nackten*] expression of self. . . . Whereas adults because of their weakening vitality, concentrate their attention more and more on the objective *contents* of life, which in the present meaning could as well be designated as its forms, youth is more concerned with the process of life (Simmel 1971:384).

Simmel's juxtaposition in this passage of the twin themes of unrestrained expression of self and positive valuation of life as process seems to imply an interpretation of Institution-Impulse/Product-Process as related, yet different dimensions.

Zurcher (1972a; 1972b; 1973) argued, in a series of papers dealing with contemporary adaptations to social change, that accelerated sociocultural change could influence a modification in the self-concept of the adapting individual. "The modification represents a significant shift, for the individual, from orientation toward stability of self (self as object) to orientation toward change of self (self as process)" (Zurcher, 1972a:4).

Using the Twenty Statements Test (TST; a paper-and-pencil measure of self-conceptions; see Kuhn and McPartland, 1954), Zurcher found that students of the 1970s made a majority of "C" statements describing personal traits and qualities or modes of expression and feeling. This represented a change from the 1950s, when respondents made primarily "B" statements identifying the self clearly and specifically with institutionalized statuses or roles. Zurcher suggested that a "B" mode self-conception, representing a self drawn from and dependent on identification with social structures, was not functional or adaptive when such institutional scaffolding was unstable, or lacked legitimacy, or was perceived as such. A "C" mode self-conception, however, "representing a self which is less dependent upon identification with social structure, is functional when that structure is undergoing rapid change" (Zurcher, 1972a:7).

Subsequent to these statements, Zurcher formulated a more complete accounting of the new self in his book *The Mutable Self: A Self-Concept for Social Change* (1977). He argued that a reflective ("C" mode) self-concept was a response to instability in the relatively stable roles and social structures upon which a social ("B" mode) self was based. Such instability could be brought about by societal change, by disruption of supporting values and rewards, by obsolescence, by personal reflection, or by conflict within the larger social system. The reflective self did not represent an endpoint, but marked the beginning of a search for new sources of self-definition. If the conditions which generated the reflective self were sustained and sufficiently repetitive, and if the person had experienced the four components of self (physical, social, reflective, oceanic), then a self-concept fully consonant with change might eventually emerge.

The Mutable Self is a self-concept which affords the individual: full recognition of the four components of self (physical, social, reflective and oceanic) and, consequently, an openness to the widest possible experience of self; an awareness of the interaction among the four components of self in varying social settings; an awareness of the process experience as well the content changes within and among the four components; the flexibility to move among the four components, willfully, purposefully, naturally, without rigid fixation on any component; the ability to integrate the four components and to accept the productive dialectic among them, a dialectic which provokes personal growth; an understanding, tolerance, acceptance of, and empathy with other human beings who manifest Mutable Selves, and for those who do not; the ability to accommodate, control or resist rapid socio-cultural change, and its concomitants, without the necessity for affecting defensive stances in, or denial of any of the four components of self (Zurcher, 1977:35–36).

Flexibility, tolerance, openness, and diversity were themes which characterized the Mutable Self. The sense of identity came not from any one activity or orientation, but from a sense of self as a continuous becoming; a becoming that did not have an end but rather was an end, to use the expression of John Dewey (1916 work, see Chapter 4).

Zurcher's serendipitous finding that patterns of TST responses had changed significantly in recent years, at least among student populations, was seconded by Sheinberg (1974), Spitzer and Parker (1976), and Snow and Phillips (1982).

Few investigators familiar with the Twenty Statements Test (TST) could fail to notice the change in response patterns over the past two decades. When the present version of the instrument appeared in 1950, populations tended to describe themselves according to membership in social groups and categories (social anchorage components) without extensive reference to individual qualifications. Now a converse pattern appears to be more characteristic. Nonconsensual statements have become predominant over consensual statements within populations which have matured over the last decade (Spitzer and Parker, 1976:236).

Zurcher also found the TSTs of dissident priests (Schneider and Zurcher, 1970) and paroled felons (Erickson et al., 1973) contained a majority of "C" statements. The paroled ex-felons and dissident priests shared at least one common characteristic—the experience of momentous change. "The dissident priests had been dislodged, by their own active protests, from the church social structure in which they had previously invested self-definition. The parolees had recently been dislodged, though not necessarily by their own acts, from prison social structure which had invested them with a self-definition" (Zurcher, 1977:53). The fact that these studies of individuals experiencing dramatic change showed them to manifest reflective selves seemed to be consistent with the argument that accelerated sociocultural change called for an answering shift in self-definitions from self-as-object to self-as-process.

Zurcher's formulation of the Mutable Self has a dominant concern with flexibility, openness, and especially the idea of *process*. Lifton's Protean Self and the Mutable Self, as well as Simmel's characterization of the experience of modern life, all share an observation of the modern self as the opposite of static, and the embodiment of change and process.

4

New Culture and Overdeveloped Modernism

We have termed *new culture* arguments those speculations about the postmodern self which focus more on general values than on the phenomenology of selfhood per se. We consider these discussions in historical order distinguishing between the "counterculture" which had taken shape by the 1970s, and more recent arguments about "new rules."

COUNTERCULTURE

The counterculture is based on the judgment that contemporary society is contrary to human needs and produces alienation from self, from other persons, and from nature. The counterculture is centered around a critique and reaction to the objective, rational, and technological values that characterize industrial society. Descriptions and arguments for the advent of the counterculture resemble new self arguments in that: (1) they describe the emergence of a qualitatively different kind of self and value system; and (2) the content of this emerging world-view and conception of the person includes ideas of the acceptance of impulse and of gratification, the full expression of emotion, the experience of the nonrational, the charismatic, and the transcendendent. Accounts and descriptions of the counterculture include those by Keniston (1965; 1968), Roszak (1969), Reich (1970), and Slater (1970). Keniston's study of alienated students preceded and in large part anticipated the counterculture movement which surfaced in the late 1960s (Keniston's preliminary work on the "uncommitted" was published in 1960).

Keniston described a "new" alienation in American society, of new origins and manifesting new form. Its origins lay in the new technological and postindustrial society that the United States had become, and its forms bore a particular relation to such a society, namely, "rebellion without a cause, . . . rejection without a program, . . . refusal of what is without a vision of what should be" (Keniston, 1965:3).

Keniston called the alienated the "uncommitted," emphasizing their lack of firm ideology or basis for belief. The uncommitted did not define themselves in terms of their social relationships or intellectual interests. On the contrary, their self-conceptions and values were vague and undefined, and they experienced themselves as "diffused, fragmented, torn in different directions by inner and outer pulls" (Keniston, 1965:162).

Many of the values and orientations of the uncommitted described by Keniston correspond to Impulse and Process categories. There was an emphasis on increased responsiveness—on genuine feeling, direct passion, pure impulse, and uncensored fantasy. The alienated were focused on the present as the locus of reality. They tried to be more receptive to new experience, more open to novel stimuli, more aware and more appreciative of their surroundings. The Impulse categories of sensory experience, emotion, feeling and passion, fantasy and present time are suggested. Keniston noted that the alienated were not able to articulate a set of positive values that they held dear. Rather, they were trying to discover positive values, a search he called the "aesthetic quest." The aesthetic quest was an attempt to "arrive at a view of the world in which experience, feeling, sentinence, passion, and appreciation" were central values (Keniston, 1965:168).

Keniston explained the alienation of the young college students as part of a more general social problem of modern American society. Succinctly stated, his argument was that "alienation is a response by selectively predisposed individuals to dilemmas and problems that confront our entire society" (Keniston, 1965:179). The overriding cause underlying these problems was an unquestioned and absolute primacy of technology, along with the technological values of specialization, organization, efficiency, rising role requirements, and innovation (Keniston, 1965:364–365). Chronic and unrestrained social change, increasing division and fragmentation of work, community, and life, and intellectualization and debunking of positive and religious values were all bound up in the unquestioned supremacy of technology. Technological values as such were not detrimental, but became so when used as supreme arbiters.

Judgments of skill, competence, and effectiveness have replaced usefulness, beauty, and relevance to human needs as criteria of worth; instrumental values have replaced final purposes; and cognitive skills have replaced virtuous character as standards of human value. . . . The human problems in our society stem not from the fact of technology, but from the supreme place we assign it in our lives (Keniston, 1965:365).

Roszak (1969:42) described the emergence of an amorphous dissent movement so much in opposition to the prevailing rational and objectivist culture of the technocratic society that he termed it a "counterculture." The new movement was a cultural rather than a political phenomenon. Its hallmark was a belief about revoking industrial and technological society by psychic rather than social means. The counterculture struck beyond political and intellectual ideology and sought to transform the deepest sense of self, the other, and the environment (Roszak, 1969:49). The reality of the technocratic rational ego—a purely cerebral entity—was assaulted, and the primacy of the non-intellectual powers was asserted.

Roszak's descriptions of the counterculture compare to the Impulse and Process categories of sense experience, emotion, irrationality, confusion and uncertainty, change, multiplicity, discovery, and present time. He described a dominant concern with the inner dimension of experience, as opposed to the outer and objective. The counterculture was grounded in an intensive examination of self and experience of the person. In this assault of the old, and grounding of the new consciousness, mystical transcendence and drug experience were accepted as means for instituting the new society. The outer world was not to be ignored but transformed by a "renewal of the mind." Social relationships as well as personal experience were to be intensively examined always with the goal of furthering the formation of new values, new experience, and new social relationships that would enhance, rather than bar, self-actualization and self-fulfillment.

In addition to campaigning for change, becoming, and self-actualization—all Process themes—the counterculture scrapped the prejudice of the rationalistic, technocratic culture against myth, religion, and ritual. It was not the institutionalized sacred that was valued, but rather the charismatic, the mystic, the occult, and the magical. The aim was not so much for religion or ritual as for religious experience: here was simply another area for discovery and actualization of self.

In a similar manner to Roszak, Reich (1970) described a new outlook, world-view, or "total configuration" that was emerging mainly but not exclusively among youth as a response to the depersonalization, meaninglessness, and repression that was felt to characterize the modern technologically based "corporate state." The new world-view ("Consciousness III") represented a radical break with the consciousness of the corporate state ("Consciousness I"). Reich emphasized the lifting of restraints against impulse and the formation of an identity oriented toward becoming, toward a present orientation.

Consciousness III meant, in essence, a recovery of self, a recovery of the personal and full experience of one's commonality with others, and of one's uniqueness as an individual. "In contrast to Consciousness II, which accepts society, the public interest, and institutions as the primary reality, III declares that the individual self is the only true reality" (Reich, 1970:241–242). The new self was to be based on the ideal of personal fulfillment and individual actualization of potentialities. The ideals for self-actualization of the older consciousness were represented by success in performing societal roles or in social acceptance. By contrast, Consciousness III said, "I'm glad I'm me" (Reich, 1970:235).

Other characteristics of the new consciousness were a devotion to the completeness and wholeness of life, an openness to experience (especially new experience), and a focus on the present and awareness of its complete potential. Energy, said Reich (1970:251), united all aspects of the new self, energy drawn "from the group, the community, from eros, from the freedom of technology, from the uninhibited self."

Reich described the multiplicity and changeableness of Consciousness III: the new self involved an insistence that the individual was not undimensional but multidimensional. "[A] single individual may do many different things in the course of a day, he is not limited to a single role or a role-plus-recreation; each individual is truly protean, with unlimited possibilities including the possibility of whatever new and spontaneous thing may come along" (Reich, 1970:253). There was also a new acceptance of the body. The body was considered not an appendage or piece of baggage but an integral part of the self. Clothing should express and reveal the individuality of the body rather than conceal it.

Rejection of the reality and the self imposed by the corporate state were expressed in rejection of success goals measured by money and status. Consciousness III considered most work available in the corporate state to be meaningless, degrading, and inconsistent with self-realization (Reich, 1970:260). However, Consciousness III was by no means lazy and would show an excess of zeal in work and activity (e.g., playing a musical instrument, working on a communal farm, constructing crafts) that was seen as contributing to self-actualization. Along with the rejection of the success values of the corporate state came a rejection of rationality, and a suspicion and distrust of linear and logical thought. Psychedelic drugs were used to aid Consciousness III in breaking out of the common ways of logical and rational thinking.

Reich's formulations about Consciousness III broke no new ground but included more Impulse and Process themes than did Roszak's, including rejection of societal duty, personal fulfillment and self-actualization, focus on the present, discovery, multiplicity and change, and rejection of material success goals.

Slater (1970:97) described a new culture emerging in the United States that he called a "protean counterculture": a new way of looking at the world based on the basic premise of non-scarcity in contradistinction to the old culture which was a "scarcity-oriented technological culture." The old culture was based on scarcity, and assumed "there just isn't enough to go around." From this basic assumption it followed that there must be a war of "all against all" and that those who could take possession and control of the largest share of scarce resources would be successful (Slater, 1970:103). By contrast, "The new culture is based on the assumption that important human needs are easily satisfied and that the resources for doing so are plentiful. Competition is unnecessary and the only danger to humans is human aggression. There is no reason outside of human perversity for peace not to reign and for life not to be spent in the cultivation of joy and beauty" (Slater, 1970:103–104).

The scarcity assumption in the old culture led to a high emphasis, Slater explained, on delayed gratification: in light of the Malthusian problem the old culture emphasized production in the present and consumption in the future. Along these same lines, the old culture emphasized restraint and viewed any stimulus arousal with fear and distrust: motivation yes, but arousal and gratification no. The new culture assumed, on the other hand, that gratification was easy and resources plentiful. Thus, stimulation was not feared but welcomed and indeed sought after.

Slater noted that an "almost infinite" number of contrasts could be drawn between the old and the new cultures. Nonetheless, the new could be differentiated from the old by the polarities of personal rights over property rights, human needs over technological requirements, cooperation over competition, sexuality over violence, distribution over concentration, consumer over producer, ends over means, openness over secrecy, personal expression over social forms, and gratification over striving (Slater, 1970:100). In drawing these contrasts, Slater pointed out that the new culture was amorphous and to an extent only took on a shape when contrasted with the old.

NEW RULES

According to some observers, the basic themes and concerns of the counterculture are today manifest in the larger population. Yankelovich (1981) noted that the "ethic of self-fulfillment" had its beginnings among college youth in the 1960s but gradually became diffused throughout American society in the 1970s by means of the women's movement, environmental and quality of life movements, and through changes in family arrangements and sexual behavior. Clecak (1983) saw the quest for personal fulfillment as the central cultural theme of the 1960s and 1970s and in more traditional forms, the following years as well.

Yankelovich described the emergence in American society of a new form of "psychoculture"—those aspects of culture concerned with shared meanings about the relationship of the person to kin and community, and with consciousness and "inner processes" (1981:14). The emergence of a new form of psychoculture amounted to no less than a "cultural revolution" in the sense that it was built upon principles and rules standing in marked contrast to those of the past, and that it impacted upon a majority of Americans.

The "ethic of self-fulfillment" was the name given to the new rules for living that were either wholeheartedly embraced or regarded sympathetically by as many as 80 percent of all adult Americans. Yankelovich's description of the ethic of self-fulfillment contained both Process and Impulse themes. But the most central principle in the new rules was a reversal in the orientation of the individual toward family and society. Traditional values proclaimed "deny thyself for the sake of others"; the new rules were "fulfill thyself" (Yankelovich, 1981:111). Paraphrasing case material, Yankelovich (1981:9) described the traditional ethic of self-denial: "I give hard work, loyalty and steadfastness. I swallow my frustrations and suppress my impulse to do what I would enjoy, and do what is expected of me instead. I do not put myself first; I put the needs of others ahead of my own."

By contrast, the ethic of self-fulfillment was to develop, cultivate, seek, and discover the self. The search for self-fulfillment was conceived as a process rather than as the attaining of specific achievements, such as money earned, possessions owned, or status achieved (Yankelovich, 1981:73). Further, the search for self-fulfillment involved greater sexual freedom, a more indulgent attitude toward different modes of sensual experience, and an appreciation of the inherent value of the domain of the expressive as opposed to the instrumental.

The ultimate cause underlying the emergence of the ethic of self-fulfillment was a fundamental and longtime contradiction in industrial society. Yankelovich cited Marx and especially Weber's analysis of the conflict between the instrumentality and rationality of Western industrial society, and the needs of human beings for community and meaning. Seekers of self-fulfillment confronted that contradiction directly.

OVERDEVELOPED MODERNISM

The overdeveloped modernism argument describes the appearance and increase of Process and Impulse themes in art, among youth, and in the larger culture. Unlike the counterculture and new self arguments, overdeveloped modernism explains that shifts in contemporary culture reacting against and criticizing rational and bureaucratic ideals and values paradoxically represent the full development of these very same trends. The warm embracement of the processual and antinomian self by contemporary culture represents the "overripe stage" of seeds planted by the industrial revolution. Replacement of a culture linked with an agricultural economy by one tied to an industrial manufacturing economy has culminated in a postmodern culture idealizing impulse and process.

Bell (1976:xxiv) "forecasted" the emergence of post-industrial society in the next thirty to fifty years that would be "in principle" different from preindustrial and industrial society by virtue of its structural basis— an intellectual technology emphasizing the major role of information and knowledge. A postindustrial economy was shaped around the formulation and dissemination of information and theoretical knowledge, as opposed to preindustrial and industrial society which were based on extractive and fabricating economies. Postindustrial society could be contrasted with industrial society by virtue of the fact that (1) it was based on an intellectual rather than a machine technology, and (2) its major structural feature was information and knowledge as opposed to capital and labor (see also Toffler, 1980).

Along with the centrality of theoretical knowledge, the other major component of postindustrial society was the expansion of the service sector as against the manufacturing sector of the economy. The term *postindustrial* referred primarily to changes in social structure (the techno-economic order), "and only indirectly to those in the polity and the culture, which comprise the other major realms of societal structure" (Bell, 1976:xxi).

Bell's ideas about the nature of cultural change in advanced industrial society were framed in terms of a conflict between social structure and culture. He saw a major problem developing in postindustrial society, a contradiction or lack of congruence between the social structure and the culture, a continuation of a trend which began in industrial society. "[W]hat has been happening in Western society for the past hundred years, I believe, is a widening disjunction between the social structure (the economy, technology, and occupational system) and the culture (the symbolic expression of meanings), each of which is ruled by a different axial principle" (Bell, 1976:477).

The substance of this contradiction was the clash of rationality, the axial principle of the social structure, with the antinomian principle of the culture. "The social structure is rooted in functional rationality and efficiency, the culture in the antinomian justification of the enhancement of the self" (Bell, 1976:477).

Bell described the rational spirit of capitalist industrial social structure in terms of its "life-style" shaped "by the principle of calculation, the rationalization of work and of time, and a linear sense of progress" (1976:477). This life-style was derived from an effort to master nature by technology, "to substitute wholly new rhythms of life for those bound to the regularities of the season and the diminishing returns of the soil" (1976:477). The principle of technical mastery was in turn "fused with a character structure which accepted the idea of delayed gratification, of compulsive dedication to work, of frugality and sobriety, and which was sanctified by the morality of service to God and the proof of self-worth through the idea of respectability" (1976:477).

Bell (1976:478) described the antinomian spirit of modernist culture in terms of its insistence on creaturehood and reality of the body, its denial of the future and exaltation of the present. Above all, modern culture was based on the principle of the development and actualization of the individual self. "[T]he axial principle of modern culture is the expression and remaking of the 'self' in order to achieve self-realization and self-fulfillment. And in its search, there is a denial of any limits or boundaries to experience. It is a reaching out for all experience; nothing is forbidden, all is to be explored" (Bell, 1978:13–14).

Bell stressed the radical subjectivity of the antinomian; it was an impulse-oriented self that was also focused on the present and on the process of life. Like Adler, he employed a term found usually in religious dialogue and called postindustrial culture *antinomian*. Likewise, he argued that the antinomian counterculture was not exclusively of contemporary origins.

Bell argued that the counterculture was not so much a contemporary phenomenon as a product of the continued advance and extension of the cultural elements that made up "modernism."

The counter-culture is a revolution in life-style which sanctions the acting-out of impulse, the exploration of fantasy, the search for polymorphic pleasure in the name of liberation from restraint. It proclaims itself "daring" and in revolt against bourgeois society. But in fact bourgeois culture vanished long ago. What the counter-culture has done is to extend the double tendencies of cultural modernism and capitalist marketing hedonism initiated sixty years ago (Bell, 1976:479).

The counterculture, and contemporary cultural themes of Impulse and Process, were extensions of modernism rather than exceptions to it. But to understand Bell's logic here we must digress a moment and consider the subject of "modernism" in more detail. By "modernism" he meant the cultural themes of the importance and significance of the individual. The fundamental assumption of modernity, which ran through Western civilization since the sixteenth century, was that the social unit of society was the person, rather than the city, the tribe, the guild, or the group (Bell, 1978:16). As expressed in the Reformation which replaced institutional judgment with that of the individual, the ideal of the West has been the autonomous, self-determining person. Modernity gave rise to the independent and autonomous bourgeois entrepreneur, freed from the traditional ties of ascription and open to the goal of a personal identity created through individual labor and effort.

In turn, however, modernity attacked institutionalized "bourgeoisie entrepreneur" character structure, with its highly respected and controlled self that feared instinct, spontaneity, and impulse, and which promulgated delay of gratification. Thus, paradoxically, modernity eventually gave rise to an antithesis of the bourgeois. The principle of restless change, of individuation and of de-institutionalization that had been the basis for capitalism within the sphere of economics, now gave rise to the idea of the "untrammeled self" within the realm of culture.

The contemporary Impulse and Process self is the same as the "untrammeled self" of nineteenth-century romanticism, and both are variations on the theme of modernism. The untrammeled self was a self of spirit and feeling, and of transcendence. Bell quoted Byron as an exemplar of the "restless vanity" of the untrammeled self. "The great object of life is Sensation—to feel that we exist—even though in pain—it is this 'craving void' which drives us to Gaming—to Battle—to Travel—to intemperate but keenly felt pursuits of every description whose principal attraction is the agitation inseparable from their accomplishment" (Byron, quoted in Bell, 1978:17).

Bell described modernism and postmodernist culture by emphasizing its Process and Impulse ideals, including its exaltation of the present and denial of the future, its acting out and acceptance of impulse, and its liberation from restraint. It was concerned with both self-realization and with self-gratification. "In the culture there was a radical change in the meaning of the individual from a being to a self. Of equal import, there was a shift from the hold of restraint to the acceptance of impulse" (Bell, 1978:18). His description of the substance of postmodern culture echoed the concerns of many of the new self and counterculture arguments that have been discussed, but his explanation of these same cultural trends differs significantly.

Bell explained the rise of postmodern culture and the antinomian self as integrally related to the emergence of industrial society, and eventually postindustrial society. It is this explanation of postmodern culture in terms of dynamics inherent to industrial society itself (as against a qualitatively new development [new self] or a reaction in the form of a critique [counterculture]) that distinguishes Bell's account and that of Sorokin.

Sorokin (1957) set forth in an ambitious and voluminous effort a theory of social change intended to apply to the whole course of Western civilization—from the ancient civilizations of Greece and Rome to the present day. Sorokin's speculations about the future of Western culture, first formulated in the early decades of the twentieth century, contain many predictions about the eventual triumph of the ideals of Impulse and Process.

Sorokin set himself the task of explaining both the emergence and the decay of cultural forms, a study he called "sociocultural dynamics." He defined the concept of culture very broadly. Culture, in its most general sense, Sorokin defined as *"the sum total of everything which is created or modified by the conscious or unconscious activity of two or more individuals interacting with one another or conditioning one another's behavior"* (1957:2). By defining culture in this way he included a wide range of phenomena including art, technology, religion, philosophy, and even "the trace of a footstep on the sand left by a savage and seen by Robinson Crusoe . . ." (Sorokin, 1957:2).

In spite of the diversity of cultural elements there were recognizable patterns. Culture had its own forms and organization that reduced the manifold into patterns of uniformity. In order to study or analyze culture, it was necessary to understand its particular principle of organization. Sorokin recognized that all cultures were not organized to the same degree, and indeed that the complexity of organization involved varied from simple association, to indirect association, to functional integration, to logico-meaningful integration (Sorokin, 1957:4–9).

Two forms of substantive or content organization of culture existed at the highest level of abstraction (cultural supersystems). Throughout one of these, "among countless other elements, runs the predominant thought that the true or *ultimate reality is supersensory.* that the reality detected by our organs of perception is illusory" (Sorokin, 1957:14). The other form of cultural integration was based on just the opposite principle: "the only reality is that of our organs of sensory perception." Sorokin termed the two types the *ideational* and the *sensate.*

If the ideational and the sensate types were thought of as defining the endpoints of a continuum, a third type would by implication exist occupying a middle range. The third type would not be based on a different axial principle than the other two but would instead incorporate aspects of both into a balanced synthesis. Sorokin termed this third type the *idealistic.*

Sorokin recognized many contrasts between the ideational and sensate supersystems. The ideational represented rationalism and mysticism over empiricism, idealism over materialism, eternalism over temporalism, and indeterminism over determinism. It represented the ethics of absolute principles over the ethics of happiness (hedonism), and was associated with a social life of a static character as contrasted with a dynamic social life and rapid rate of change.

Contemporary culture, Sorokin thought, was undergoing a transition. Sensate culture was declining and disintegrating, having been the dominant system of culture from the fifteenth through the nineteenth centuries. The modern era was a time of crisis, as a new principle of cultural organization was gaining strength.

Many of the characteristics that Sorokin ascribed to the declining or "overripe" sensate phase called attention to the emergence of Impulse and Process values and ideals. There was an emphasis on change and experimentation. "The Sensate reality is thought of as a Becoming, Process, Change, Flux, Evolution, Progress, Transformation" (Sorokin, 1957:27). Sorokin noted that theories and philosophies of becoming had risen and become extraordinarily prevalent since the end of the eighteenth and beginning of the nineteenth century. The modern age was more and more concerned with this theme. "The category of Becoming— of change, of process, of evolution, of flux, of transformation, of mutation, of revolution—has become the fundamental category of our mentality, the specific glass through which more and more the Western society has been seeing the reality. It has been becoming blinder and blinder to the eternal or lasting aspects of it" (Sorokin 1957:317).

The category of "Becoming" was characteristically sensate, the ideology of temporalism. Temporalism stood in opposition to the ideology of being (eternalism) which stressed that the true and ultimate reality was unchanging.

The temporalistic character of the advanced sensate was expressed by a focus on the present. "By definition, temporalism is centered in the present. Remote past is over; remote future is uncertain. Only the present moment of the endless flux is real, only it exists and only it has value" (Sorokin, 1957:319).

A consequence of the increasing temporalism and emphasis on the present was an accelerating pace of social life, a faster rhythm of social change. "Tempo of change has increased already to a maddening speed in the turnover of all our values, from the changing models of our cars, radios, clothing, buildings, to the turnover in husbands and wives, mores, best sellers, art styles, scientific theories, philosophies, beliefs, and economic and political structures" (Sorokin, 1957:319). Fashion was the watchword of the temporalistic mentality of modern sensate culture, as opposed to the "lasting tradition" of eternalistic culture.

As a consequence of the extreme emphasis on change and flux, the ideology of temporalism resulted in an insufficient amount of time for the testing, evaluation, and appreciation of values, ideas, morals, and ways of living.

Nothing has sufficient time to crystalize. Everything is in a liquid state. Nothing has a chance to be tested for its good or bad qualities. We really do not know which of the incessantly changing "models" and values are good and which are poor. Therefore *the whole social life and the whole mentality are also in a liquid state, formless, shapeless, foggy, like a primeval protoplasm or a crowd of fleeting shadows* (Sorokin, 1957:320).

One would look in vain, wrote Sorokin, for clear-cut boundary lines between good and evil, right and wrong, true and false. A pervasive relativism resulted from the absence of general standards. Relativism in turn was associated with lack of certainty, lack of security or stability in modern social life. Confronted with the "continuous change" of sensate society, its inhabitants did their best to adjust, but their task was hopeless, "more hopeless than that of Sisyphus" (1957:320).

With those emphases on the present and continual change, Sorokin was clearly forecasting the occurrence of Process themes. But he also made a place for Impulse by pointing out that the quest to live totally in the present changing moment led to a focus on physical and emotional experience.

Sorokin explained the crisis of the modern sensate phase by outlining a general theory of sociocultural change based on the "principle of immanent change," and the "principle of limit." The principle of immanent change was that any sociocultural system changes "by virtue of its own forces and properties. *It cannot help changing, even if all its external conditions are constant*" (Sorokin, 1957:633). Sociocultural systems change because it cannot be otherwise with active and functioning systems.

The principle of limit meant that sociocultural systems had finite possibilities for change. For a great number of sociocultural systems, if not for all, linear evolution was not possible. They could move now in one direction and reach a limit, but would then have to turn to a new path. A system that possessed unlimited possibilities for change could become anything; it might even become radically different and unidentifiable from its previous state. A change this radical would be "equivalent to the cessation of the existence of the system and to its replacement by another—quite different—system. For these almost axiomatic reasons, practically any system must have and does have limits to the range of its change" (Sorokin, 1957:654). The principle of limit applied to the main types of society, to sociocultural systems, and to sociocultural processes.

The principles of immanent change and of limit explained the rise and fall of Ideational, Idealistic, and Sensate cultures, including the crisis of the sensate of our own contemporary era. "*By virtue of the principle of immanent change, each of the three integrated forms, or phases, of the Ideational, Idealistic and Sensate supersystems cannot help changing; rising, growing, ex-*

isting full-blooded for some time, and then declining" (Sorokin, 1957:676).

In other words, each of the major types of cultural organization bore within itself the seeds of its own destruction. Each system of "truth" was to an extent inadequate and incomplete and would have to eventually recognize the truth of the opposing principles. If one supersystem achieved complete dominance over the others, it would necessarily be replaced eventually as an outcome of its very success. However, a sociocultural supersystem that compromised and admitted the truth of the others would continue to function to the extent that a viable synthesis of the opposing principles was achieved.

The crisis of twentieth-century culture was the crisis of a culture that refused to recognize any truth except that of the senses. The contemporary era was a time of transition between a waning sensate supersystem that had already reached its zenith and a new ideational or idealistic order. It was the "crisis of a Sensate culture, now in its overripe stage . . . " (Sorokin, 1957:622). A culture that had dominated the Western world during the last five centuries was now entering its period of decline and eventual demise.

SIMILAR AND RELATED DISCUSSIONS

Several social scientists, philosophers, and social observers have described similar or related distinctions to Institution-Impulse and Product-Process. Some in addition note that a shift is (or will be) occurring among modern populations.

Freud (see e.g., 1965; also Strachey, 1962) differentiated between the instinctual aspect of personality (biological) and regulating or moral components (societal). Although it was to be in the ultimate service of ego, Freud did call for more recognition of the id in personality ("Where id was there ego shall be").

Jung indicated the alienation and dehumanization that resulted from ego's (the conscious mind's) identification with the *persona*—the public, conventional, role-playing side of personality (Campbell, 1971). Jung saw psychological development as a process of assimilation from the public and conscious toward the unconscious—toward the realization of *self* as a balance of all aspects of personality (thinking, feeling, sensing, intuiting).

"Third stream" American psychologists also emphasized the positive consequences of self based more on personal than public experience, and furthermore called for a self more open to change and reconstruction. Maslow (1969:50–51), commenting on similarities between the European existential psychology and trends in American psychology (e.g., self-psychologies, growth psychologies, self-actualization psychologies), noted that (1) there has been a "total collapse of all sources of values outside the individual," and (2) "There is no place else to turn but inward, to the self, as the locus of values." This shift to the self as a source of values could result in the emergence of the "authentic person" who transcends his or her culture, and who "becomes a little more a member of his species and a little less a member of his local group" (Maslow, 1969:52).

Rogers (1969) described the valuing process (rather than value system) characteristic of the mature person. Most persons lived by a closed system of values, derived not from their own experience but from without, and not subject to re-evaluation or revision. The mature person in contrast manifested a "valuing process," in which values were continually adopted and recast based on the experience of personal growth and self-actualizations.

Emphasizing continuous reconstruction over fixed goals in a very similar manner, Dewey (1916:49–50) criticized those who regarded education—and growth in general—as having an end rather than being an end.

When it said that education is development, everything depends upon *how* development is conceived. Our net conclusion is that life is development, and that developing, growing, is life. Translated into its educational equivalents, that means (i) that the educational process has no end beyond itself; it is its own end; and that (ii) the educational process is one of continual reorganizing, reconstructing, transforming.

Dewey later (1922) applied this same critique to the notion of self as a fixed entity.[1] Along similar lines, Fromm (1972) described the flawed identity that resulted from an experience of self based on having rather than being.

Lynd (1968) differentiated between guilt-related identity, and identity based on shame. The former meant an identity drawn from and grounded in customs, mores, and the prescribed ways of life of one's group. Identity built upon shame, however, meant a self based on a more personal way of life, usually reflecting allegiance to values and standards transcending the boundaries of one's caste and class. Shame identity required continual reappraisal and reconsideration or accepted and approved ways of life in light of more transcendent ideals. Identity had to be realized not through a series of discrete acts, but through a lifelong process of change and discovery.

In the field of literature, Trilling (1972) described shifting modes of self-consciousness and moral life in Western culture under the headings of sincerity and authenticity. As the European feudal order dissolved and the authority of the church diminished, "society" and "individual" took on more modern meanings and the ideal of sincerity emerged. Sincerity meant being true to one's self for the purpose of being true to others; through the virtue of sincerity the social order was upheld and the individual granted the just desserts of esteem and public regard. By contrast, the modern virtue of authenticity influenced people to cast a jaundiced eye at self-encounter in the service of the social order. Instead, self-discovery and self-realization were urged as ends in themselves (hence the modern concept of self-actualization; see Maslow, 1962, and Rogers, 1972) Trilling traced the emergence of the ideal of authenticity in the writings of Hegel, Marx, Nietzsche, and Conrad.

Of special relevance to the present study are Fothergill's observations about different forms of self-consciousness drawn from his study of English diaries. Fothergill (1974:128–129) distinguished between diarists who projected an object self (a Product to be accomplished) and those who viewed selfhood in terms of Process (multiple roles and ways of action).

Many people and many diarists never seriously encounter the questions, What am I really like? In what directions would I wish to change myself? What am I becoming? What might I make of myself? In the concerns of those who do, two intersecting perspectives reveal themselves, a vertical and a horizontal axis, so to speak. From one perspective the concern is expressed as the struggle toward a goal, a stage of self-development envisaged as superior to one's present condition. The alternate perspective views self-hood in terms of singleness and multiplicity, identity being realizable either as the one authentic role among two or more contestants, or as a complex unity of dual or multiple aspects. In these latter terms, which tend to prevail in the self-consciousness articulated in diaries of the nineteenth and twentieth centuries, the predominant concern is to explore and be reconciled with the complexities of one's nature.

NOTE

1. See Thayer (1968:174–183) for a discussion of the centrality of growth and continuity in Dewey's philosophy.

5

The Challenge of Studying Self and Social Change

Theories describing the emergence of a postmodern self carry the implication of changes in family arrangements, work roles, and in other social institutions as well. In view of the significance of such changes, a reasonable question to ask is: "What is the evidence for the claims made?" Given the richness of the theoretical enterprise, the answer is surprising. Theories of a postmodern self have been advanced in the context of little to no empirical evidence.[1] Having discussed the what and why of the postmodern self, we turn now to the complementary questions of how and when.

Several lines of similarity, and divergence, are evident among postmodern self arguments. There is general agreement about the content of change, which has been expressed in terms of the Institution-Impulse/Product-Process theoretical dimensions. While not always stated explicitly, it is usually implied in these arguments that Institution and Product themes are declining in some proportion to the waxing of Process and Impulse themes, and that these shifts are taking place for the most part in the United States.

There is a lack of agreement concerning the time frame of the shift to the postmodern, and even less consensus about explanations of the emergence of the postmodern self. Concerning the time dimension, Adler believed the antinomian to be unrelated to the uniqueness of the present historical context. The antinomian appeared many times in the past and would so again during times of instability and crisis. Kavolis' viewpoint was that "psychological modernization" (which began as early as the seventeenth century) resulted in two opposing forms of personality and culture (modern versus underground), that nevertheless differed in content according to the particular social situation of the period in question. Kavolis, by his citations of late 1960 counterculture figures (e.g., Leary, 1968), seemed to have in mind fairly recent times as the fabricator of the distinctively contemporary underground type. Turner (1976:990) warned against overlooking more extended historical trends. This caveat was consonant with his citation of such nineteenth-century figures as William Wordsworth. Lifton (1968:115) identified the protean pattern as characteristic of "contemporary life," and cited Sartre (born 1905) as the "embodiment of twentieth-century man" (1968:118). Simmel (1971:380), commenting on the contemporary scene (1914), wrote: "I will now illustrate through several contemporary examples the uniqueness of the cultural situation we are undergoing, in which the longing for a new form always overturns the old one, in particular, the opposition against the principle of form as such." Zurcher (1977) envisioned the Mutable Self as a phenomenon of near future rather than the immediate present, though a self resembling it could be found presently in some subcultures and in some individuals.

Among those representative discussions of the counterculture considered above, all more or less agreed on the late 1960s as the time of the emergence of this movement, although as Keniston's studies showed, the themes which characterized the counterculture also characterized the feelings of many young persons in the years immediately preceding the 1960s.

The overdeveloped modernism arguments posited a more complex explanation: the content of twentieth-century contemporary culture was both unique and part of a recurrent cycle. Bell differed from Sorokin somewhat in that Bell identified the beginning of the dialectic between rationalist modernism and antinomian modernism not in ancient civilization, but in Western capitalist industrial society.

If postmodern self arguments were ambiguous or vague concerning the time of emergence of the postmodern, they were virtually silent on a crucial point: the time of development of the Institution and Product self, which provides the touchstone for the postmodern. While at least some pilot preliminary or anecdotal evidence is provided for the postmodern, there is virtual absence of even that with regard to the presupposed "modern" self. Which aspects of the Institution and Product self are modern, that is, associated with industrial revolution and modernization? Which aspects are premodern, or in existence before a modern self? The statements forecasting the emergence of a postmodern self highlight the fact that empirically based sociological knowledge of a historically prior "modern" self is problematic. Because of the different perspectives about the "when" of the emergence of the postmodern self, and the lack of explicit consideration about the preceding modern self, an attempt to gather evidence about the postmodern must consider its historical origins and content prior to the latter twentieth century.

Taken together, there are at least three perspectives concerning the time dimension of the postmodern self: (1) it is a uniquely contemporary phenomenon, related to the continued historical development of industrial society; (2) it is largely independent of historical situation and has been manifested in the past as well as the present; and (3) it is occurring in the present as a result of conditions (e.g., rapid sociocultural change) that are generally, but not necessarily, associated with contemporary life. In spite of the different perspectives about the time dimension, none of the works reviewed here would seem to contradict the statements that themes of Impulse and Process began to emerge in art at least by the beginning of the nineteenth century, and these themes have increasingly become manifest in the culture of twentieth-century industrial society.

The agreement among the three basic perspectives on the postmodern self can be summarized as follows:

1. A set of changes is now occurring in cultural forms of identity and self-concept in the United States, which began with cultural shifts in the nineteenth century.

2. These changes can be represented as an increase in the frequency and importance of Impulse themes and Process themes relative to Institution and Product themes.

The explanations posed by the various observations of postmodern shifts in cultural forms of self and identity are more difficult to categorize neatly than were the perspectives on time, and indeed, there seem to be as many explanations for the phenomenon as there are observers of it. The explanations posed in the works identified for discussion explaining the emergence of the new self are: (1) a reaction to the successful rationalization and secularization of industrial society (Kavolis, Turner, Keniston); (2) a consequence of accelerated social change (Adler, Zurcher, Keniston); (3) a result of the weakening (or perceived weakening) of secular and rational institutions (Turner); (4) a result of increasing importance of consumption over production values and orientations (Turner); (5) a consequence of the decline of the sense of historical continuity associated with secularization and modernization of society (Lifton); (6) a symbolic overload due to a rapid increase or flooding of cultural imagery (Lifton); (7) a struggle of the process of life against the principle of cultural form (Simmel); and (8) the "overripe" development of secular and rationalistic Western culture (Sorokin).

The diversity of explanations about the emerging postmodern self highlights the lack of clear consensus about the time dimensions of the phenomenon, and underscores the need for empirical grounding of these ideas. Having accomplished the theoretical work of determining limits and imposing structure on the ideas collectively comprising the hypothesis of the postmodern self, we now turn to the task of empirical work: specifying a research methodology for our exploratory study.

Despite neglect by sociologists and other social observers interested in historical and contemporary change in forms of self-concept and identity, a rich source of data is available which allows comparative study of contemporary individuals with those from the past. We consider the use of personal documents, especially personal journals or diaries, as a data source in the following chapter.

NOTE

1. Sorokin's work is a notable exception.

6

The Use of Personal
Documents in Social Science
Research

HISTORICAL PERSPECTIVES

Records and written documents containing accounts of individual experience were used enthusiastically by American sociologists during the early development of sociology, especially by the "Chicago School" in the 1920s and 1930s.[1] Studies conducted during this period using autobiographies, life-histories, diaries, letters, essays, and other personal documents included such classics as Thomas and Znaniecki's *The Polish Peasant in Europe and America* (1958), Park and Miller's *Old World Traits Transplanted* (1921), Zorbaugh's *The Gold Coast and the Slum* (1929), Thrasher's *The Gang* (1927), and Shaw's *The Jack Roller* (1930). Cavan (1929) published a review of studies based on life-history (case study) material in the *American Journal of Sociology* from 1920 to 1929. She found seventy-five publications employing this technique, including contributions from psychologists, lawyers, priests, and social workers.

During its heyday, the use of personal documents was linked to the methodology of the case study. Hinkle (1951) noted in her study of the influence of Freud on American sociology that although American sociologists had rejected the Freudian sex instinct, they accepted the essentials of the psychoanalytic method by way of the "life-history" method. It is important to note that life-histories, personal documents, and other case materials were analyzed qualitatively. The life-history method was directly related to what came to be known as the method of participant observation. The strong naturalistic and holistic bent of the early Chicago School found its expression in these characteristic methods of social research.

The strongest case for the use of personal documents in sociology was made by Thomas and Znaniecki, who said in the introduction to part 4 of *The Polish Peasant* (1958:1832–1833):

We are safe in saying that personal life-records, as complete as possible, constitute the *perfect* type of sociological material, and that if social science has to use other materials at all it is only because of the practical difficulty of obtaining at the moment a sufficient number of such records to cover the totality of sociological problems, and of the enormous amount of work demanded for an adequate analysis of all the personal materials necessary to characterize the life of a social group.

The life-history method and the use of personal documents attracted serious criticism despite the enthusiastic acclaim it received from supporters such as Thomas and Znaniecki. Blumer, in a critique (1939) of Thomas and Znaniecki's use of "human documents" in their study of the Polish peasant, noted four criteria of evaluation.[2] These criteria were representativeness, adequacy, reliability, and validity of interpretation. Blumer argued that Thomas and Znaniecki gave no proof of their assertion about the representativeness of the documents. He called into question the adequacy of the documents as complete and comprehensive statements. He questioned the reliability of the documents, and their truthfulness and sincerity. He suggested the possibility that they contained "dressed up" accounts in view of a particular audience. Blumer also raised the question of the accuracy of memory of the autobiographical writers. Finally, he questioned the validity of the interpretations that Thomas and Znaniecki drew on the basis of their analysis of the documents.

Objections to the use of personal documents similar to those of Blumer were listed by Allport (1942) in the second of the Social Science Research Council (SSRC) methodological studies of personal documents (Blumer's critique was the first). Allport identified the most serious criticisms of the use of personal documents in psychological science as: (1) the problem of obtaining a representative sample; (2) the problems of oversimplification, blindness to motives, self-justification, deception, and self-deception—factors all related to the effect of the individual's observation of his or her own behavior and thoughts; and (3) the problem of validity of the linkages made between empirical data and theory.

Although Allport's work was supplemented by a third publication sponsored by the SSRC on the use of personal documents in history, anthropology, and sociology (Gottschalk et al., 1945), his remained the best single discussion of the advantages and disadvantages of such data.

The scarcity of serious methodological discussions of the use of personal documents in the years following the last of the Social Science Research Council publications bears witness to the decline of their use in American sociology. Among the few post–Social Science Research Council methodological discussions of personal documents that did appear, little or no reference to new evidence was included.[3] Over the years, the personal document as data was submitted to quantification and control as social researchers attempted to become more objective in their methods. Eventually such first-person autobiographical material as the life-history came to be considered not as a special subfield, but as part of the more general method of the open-ended or projective interview (Madge, 1962).

More recently there has been a resurgence of interest in personal documents as part of a larger concern with the use of qualitative methods.[4] A reading of these sources, however (e.g., Bogdan and Taylor, 1975; Bouchard, 1976; Mariampolski and Hughes, 1978; Bertaux, 1981; Plummer, 1983), shows that little empirical work on questions of methodology (reliability, validity, and representativeness) has taken place since the 1930s, at least in North American sociology.[5] The main proponents and active users of personal documents in sociology today (as opposed to the early decades of the twentieth century) appear to be European and especially Polish sociologists (see, e.g., Adamski, n.d.; Bukowski, 1974; Chalasinski, 1981; Szczepanski, 1965; Viewegh, 1972).

The case against personal documents may be summarized in terms of three kinds of objections or criticisms (Madge, 1965): (1) distortion by the investigator and lack of valid inferences drawn from analysis of the document; (2) distortion by the informant; and (3) representativeness.

INVESTIGATOR DISTORTION

Considering first the problem of distortion by the investigator and validity of inferences drawn from analysis of the document, the question may be profitably considered in terms of the *context of discovery*, and the *context of verification* (Rudner, 1966). The former term refers to the invention and initiation of theories. The latter refers to their empirical testing. Critics of personal documents have had little quarrel with the use of life-histories, letters, and autobiographies to suggest "hunches" for further investigation. That is, they have not criticized their use in the context of discovery. However, the recognition of the value of such materials for discovery has often amounted to damning with faint praise.

By contrast, questions about adequacy of proof (the context of verification) have been among the most serious criticisms of personal documents. Blumer's critique of *The Polish Peasant* was a forceful statement of this criticism. He recapped his arguments (1939:108–110) in a December 1938 conference on the work held by the Committee on Appraisal of Social Research.[6] Besides W.I. Thomas and Blumer, those present included Gordon W. Allport, Read Bain, Max Lerner, George P. Murdock, Samuel A. Stouffer, Willard W. Waller, and Louis Wirth.

Thomas and Znaniecki have presented theories covering many topics, covering an enormously wide field, and the implication is that they have sought to demonstrate the validity of these theories by the use of this human documentary material. As I saw it, my task was to see to what extent this is true, and to this point I limited my appraisal. . . .
I concluded that it is inconceivable that the theoretical schemes which Thomas and Znaniecki presented in their work could have been derived from their documentary materials. . . . However, the point is not very important because it does not matter much where or how a person gets his theoretical views. The only thing that matters is whether these theoretical views can be tested by the evidence submitted. This, then, became my task, to see to what extent this was true in this particular case.
My impression is that the larger part of their theoretical interpretation, and particularly its more abstract features, cannot be tested by their documentary materials.

Blumer then described a fundamental dilemma for social research presented by *The Polish Peasant*. Thomas and Znaniecki's work demonstrated conclusively the need for recognizing and considering the "subjective factor in human experience," but it also illustrated an obstacle to the use of human documents to achieve that aim. The obstacle was the difficulty of performing a theory verification operation on the documents. Moreover, the dilemma between the necessity for considering the subjective factor and the difficulty of verifying observations of it went far beyond the limitations of personal documents. Rather, it was a more general problem posed by the nature of the subjective factor itself—it resisted the application of objective methods. Blumer saw a definite need for social research to take the definition of the situation into account, but he also believed the subjective factor was largely unresearchable with objective methods. He stated this (1939:114–115) in response to a query by Allport about the value of statistical studies relative to the use of human documents:

It seems to me we must face this point upon which Thomas and Znaniecki base their whole work, viz., the indispensable necessity of getting at the subjective element in our efforts to understand human behavior, whether it is individual or collective. I think the statistical approach will generally, though not necessarily, confine itself to what it calls objective factors, in other words, external influences playing upon human beings which can be counted, and responses which likewise can be counted. Thus, the statistical approach will tend to ignore this mediating factor of subjective experience which Thomas and Znaniecki emphasize as essential. For this reason, the statistical approach will tend to remain one-sided. If the statistician should ever grapple with the identification of this subjective factor, then we would have to face the same problem we are now discussing.

Despite Blumer's pessimism about the applicability of quantitative and statistical methods to the analysis of personal documents and language symbols, the passage of only a decade saw the initiation and development of such methods—defined collectively as *content analysis*—to a degree that made possible one of the largest and most extensive studies of political symbols and language ever undertaken. The RADIR project (Revolution and the Development of International Relations), conducted by Lasswell, de Sola Pool, Lerner, and others at the Hoover Institution from 1948 to 1953 (de Sola Pool et al., 1970), was a study of political ideas and ideology as reflected in prestige newspapers. The systematic and explicit methods of content analysis did not and do not obviate the dilemma that Blumer posed.[7] However, such methods did make possible the testing of hypotheses about symbolic material to the extent that social researchers could make explicit the ideas and concepts of interest can operationalize them into coding rules.

INFORMANT DISTORTION

The second group of criticisms of personal documents contains the common theme of distortion by the informant. Criticisms of this kind discussed by Allport included deception, self-deception, blindness to motives, oversimplification and artificial consistency, effects of mood or mood changes, and memory errors. The common theme of questions raised about informant/subject distortion is that of a gulf between words and deeds.

The problem of informant distortion is more or less consequential depending on the type of question that the research is designed to answer. The disciplines of history, sociology, and psychology can differ significantly in the nature of the questions they ask of documentary evidence. For example, historians may consult documentary records in order to answer questions about concrete historical settings in which interest centers on the actual behavior of actor A versus actor B, or on who said what to whom. An illustrative case is provided by the researches of a Texas historian about the battle of the Alamo and the fate of its heroic defenders. The publication of a diary kept by one of Santa Ana's staff revealed that Davy Crockett was actually captured and executed when the Alamo was seized on March 6, 1836, contrary to popular legend. Kilgore, in his essay "*How Did Davy Die*" (1978), explained how he became interested in the historical validity of the diary account and eventually corroborated the diarist's version of Crockett's fate through a reading of statements from other Mexican soldiers.

Similarly, psychologists are often interested in specific behaviors and the effect of particular settings on behavior. A psychologist might, for instance, be interested in researching ideas about the influence of childhood environment on later personality development, and so consult a parent's journal to help identify the actual style of socialization. One of Freud's more well-known cases, "little Hans" (1955), was an analysis of a five-year-old boy based on letters written to Freud by the boy's father. Questions dealing with the behavior of individuals and the concrete influences on such behavior call for detailed and accurate descriptions.

By contrast, a sociologist might be interested in an "account" itself, apart from its truth value as a description of social reality. Sociologists might compare accounts given by individuals from different social strata, or be interested in the variation in accounts over time. The important issue from a sociological standpoint is not whether distortion by an informant exists—it is a basic sociological assumption that perception and world-view are influenced by social position—but how much of the distortion is idiosyncratic to an individual, and how much is held in common with other individuals from similar social positions. Distortion or subject/informant bias associated with membership in social categories is one of the central phenomena with which sociology deals. For sociologists, personal documents are an invaluable source of information about individual and group values, ideals, fears, and wishes. It bears pointing out here also that, as noted by Barton (1974) in his analysis of diaries of Civil War soldiers, the same problems of subject/informant distortion that trouble social research using personal documents also interfere with social survey research.

REPRESENTATIVENESS

A third criticism of the use of diaries and personal documents in social research is that of representativeness. The issue will be considered in two parts: quantitative representativeness, and typological representativeness (Bukowski, 1974; see below). Both terms apply to the task of making inferences about social groups on the basis of less than perfect knowledge. The former is understood to mean generalization by probability sampling and statistical aggregation. The latter is understood to mean generalization through the analysis of types and typological phenomena.

Concerning statistical representativeness, the criticism is often made of personal documents that the population writing diaries and autobiographies differs significantly from the general population. It is charged that only persons with a certain social background or social status write personal documents. The available evidence on this question is sketchy, and dates largely from the 1920s and 1930s when the personal document was in its heyday in social research. Ponsonby (1923) reported that on the basis of his informal survey of "educated persons," he believed about a quarter of the adult population kept diaries. Allport (1942) cited a Russian study published in 1935 which showed that two-thirds of adolescent girls and one-third of adolescent boys kept diaries. He noted that an unpublished study in an Eastern college indicated that 71 percent of college women had kept a diary at one time, but only about 36 percent continued their diary writing. Allport also cited a Japanese study published in 1922 which showed that among 3,500 students between the ages of thirteen and twenty-one, one-half of college level students and a smaller proportion of students in the middle grades kept diaries. Allport concluded from his review of available evidence that the charge of unrepresentativeness was unconvincing.

Whatever the case with respect to diary writing in general, bibliographers and students of the diary would probably agree that most *published* diaries are written by persons with higher levels of education and from white-collar and professional occupations. However, even among published diaries there is some representation from a wide variety of backgrounds and social positions, including, for example, slaves, farmers, and even the solitary pioneering trader and trapper, the "mountain man" (Walker, 1974).[8]

In view of the statistical unrepresentativeness of the population of persons who have written published diaries, the social researcher using diaries or other personal documents to study social change should not formulate the research in terms of the logic of survey research, but should work instead from a historical reconstruction framework where generalizing to a theory is of primary interest. The difficulties of generalizing from personal documents calls for a research logic analogous to that of experiments, where generalizations are made about a theory rather than a sampling universe. Yin (1984) has contrasted the analytical generalization strategy common to experiments and case studies with the statistical generalization strategy common to survey studies.

Representativeness of personal documents can also be considered from the standpoint of *typological representativeness*. Because personal documents are or are not written by individuals who collectively are statistically representative of the larger population does not preclude their usefulness to identify common values and typical phenomena. Weber stated the strongest form of this argument with his concept of the ideal type that by definition lacks quantitative representativeness. That is to say, an ideal type is not based on an empirical enumeration and averaging procedure, but represents a "typical" case by abstraction from reality and integration of various components into a meaningful whole (Weber, 1978a:19–22; Parsons, 1968).

Arguments for typological representativeness can be considered along two lines: generalizing about group symbols and cultural phenomena, and generalizing on the basis of heightened self-reflexiveness of personal document authors. We will consider the latter issue below in a separate discussion dealing solely with characteristics of diaries.

The value of letters, diaries, and autobiographical materials for researching cultural perceptions and social values has been recognized by historians and sociologists, and by social investigators in the field of American studies as well. Berkhofer made this point about all documentary evidence. He argued that because of the relative scarcity of documentary evidence, it was easier to establish the existence of norms than individual adherence to them.

... [G]iven the scantiness of historical data, there are usually far too few documents in even the most voluminous manuscript collections to serve as evidence for a psychological appraisal of personality. On the other hand, just a few scraps of paper here and there in various individual's collections can serve to establish the nature of and conformity to the social conventions and cultural attitudes of a populace, for each additional piece of evidence testifying to a practice serves to prove that it is common to the members of a given society. Dispositions to obey societal custom are therefore far easier to prove than dispositions to individualistic psychological attributes. Accordingly, historians should direct their efforts far more than they do to seeking social and cultural interpretations of their subjects rather than the oversimplified psychology so often urged upon them (1969:62–63).

An argument for regarding autobiography not as factual truth but as a reflection of culture and mythic images of character was made by Spengemann and Lundquist (1965).[9] They argued that autobiography had little or nothing to do with "factual truth," and was also not a mode of communicating "raw experience." Rather, autobiography presented

... a metaphor for the raw experience. The language of autobiography stands in symbolic relation to both author and subject. As an author translates his life into language he creates for himself a symbolic identity and sees himself through the focusing glass of language. Since the language of the autobiographer is the common possession of his culture, it is not only subject to his personal manipulation, but it is filled with the assumed values of his society. The act of writing about oneself brings together the personal, unassimilated experiences of the writer and the shared values of his culture (Spengemann and Lundquist, 1965:502).

Shared values of American culture described by Spengemann and Lundquist included mythical images of character describing human history as a "pilgrimage from imperfection to perfection." The writing of autobiography was a "cultural act," an expression and interpretation of individual experience in terms of common mythical images of character. "In autobiography the writer explains his life by depicting himself according to culturally evaluated images of character. As he turns his private experiences into language he assumes one of the many identities outlined in the myth and so asserts his connection with his culture" (Spengemann and Lundquist, 1965:504).

A study of the language of moral evaluation and character in the diaries of Northern and Southern officers from the Civil War (Barton, 1974) pointed out the usefulness of diaries for revealing standards by which the two groups judged character. Barton was interested more in the content of the standards themselves, and in what was defined as desirable and undesirable, than in the individual diarists' adherence to the standard.

The factual accuracy of a diary—usually the main concern of historians—is not nearly so important for us as the *criteria* the diarist uses when making either true or false estimations of his own and others' character. If the diarist uses his document to boost his own ego or brag about his own qualities, thereby blocking our access to his "real" behavior, we still have a description of his "ideal self." If he inaccurately disparages or praises other persons, the same holds true—we have learned something about his "conceptions of the desirable" (Barton, 1974:248).

The argument made by Berkhofer, Spengemann and Lundquist, and Barton points to the usefulness of personal documents for researching norms, customs, and other cultural phenomena, but does not make claims for unique advantages of autobiographical material. However, such an argument can be made, and flows from a recognition of the heightened self-awareness and reflexiveness that autobiography (especially diary writing) brings about. This argument is described below.

THE SPECIAL VALUE OF DIARIES

The diary or journal is commonly understood to be a periodic or episodic written record of an individual's activities and personal experiences. Documents of this kind have been part of Western culture for several centuries, dating at least from the sixteenth century among English–speaking peoples (Ponsonby, 1923; MacFarlane, 1970).

Fothergill noted in his literary study of British diaries (1974) that more or less self-contained and autonomous diary writing (where the diary is not a by-product or off-shoot of writing undertaken with some other task in mind) coalesced from several sources. Precursors of the modern form of the diary include journals of travel, public journals such as business or military logs or records, journals of conscience where the sole preoccupation of the writer is on his or her inner moral life, and journals of personal memoranda and daily activities.

Fothergill dated the genesis of the modern "personal" diary as 1 January 1660, the date of the first entry of the journal of Samuel Pepys.[10] Fothergill argued that Pepys created the modern form of diary by focusing on his own life and experience as his sole justification for writing. Pepys' journal differed from the previous "proto-diaries" (as Fothergill termed them) by its avoidance of one-sidedness and its singular focus on the whole of an individual life.

The point about Pepys is that in his hands the "personal" diary finds, from the very first entry, a form so confident and commodious as to make preceding efforts, and those for some time to come, seem like so many false starts.... Most notably he balances the outer and inner life in a very harmonious relation to one another. In a manner which appears to be simplicity itself, but is actually very rare, he renders all his experiences, from the most public to the most private, in the same key, as it were, treating all the contents of a day impartially (Fothergill, 1974:13).

Pepys' journal included his public and private, sacred and secular life, and was a narrative of the everyday and the uncommon.

Common to many definitions of the diary are the qualities of *periodicity* and *reflexivity*. Ponsonby, editor, bibliographer, and author of several books on British diaries, defined the diary as "the daily or periodic record of personal experiences and impressions" (1923:1). Matthews, compiler of bibliographies on American (1959; 1974) and English (1950) diaries, and co-editor of the definitive edition of Pepys' diary (Latham and Matthews, 1970), defined it as "a day-by-day record of what interested the diarist, each day's record being self-contained and written shortly after the events occurred, the style being usually free from organized exposition" (1959:ix). Fothergill (1974:48) noted that a common feature of such personal documents, called "diaries" by their authors, was that they were written "in the first person as a discontinuous series of more or less self-contained responses to the writer's present situation and recent experience."

The personal journal or diary is a valuable source of data for research on self-concept and social change because it provides a format for continued personal reflexive thinking and writing, and because it has been in existence for several hundred years. The diary or journal gives both opportunity and justification for a conversation with the self, a continuing encounter between self-as-experiencer and self-as-experienced. It provides a unique format for self-confession, self-clarification, and self-realization. Having been in existence for several hundred years, the form allows for the comparative study of shared values and self-definitions of persons from different historical eras.

The *autobiography* and the *letter* are two additional forms of personal writing that allow the study of change over time in shared values, definitions of the situation, and of self. Nevertheless the autobiography and the letter have disadvantages that diaries do not have. The autobiography is written mostly from a single point in time, typically toward the end of an individual's life. A whole lifetime is interpreted from a singular historical period, and from the point of view of the endpoint of personal development. The autobiography is more likely to have been penned with the goal of publication in mind, requiring as it does a much larger commitment by the individual of time and expense. Considerations of marketability and liability inevitably would have to be taken into account by autobiographers who were considering publication—probably a majority of autobiographical authors. To point out the fact that writers of autobiography are often concerned with publication considerations is not to say that diarists are oblivious to these considerations, but that diarists write under fewer constraints along these lines than do autobiographers.

Letters escape these two objections to autobiography, but have a problem of their own. Letters are always written to a specific person or persons, at a particular stage in a relationship, in view of preceding communication and of future interaction. Other things being equal, it is reasonable to expect that letters would be subject to more situational variation than diaries or autobiographies because they are written to specific audiences with specific purposes in mind.[11]

REFLEXIVITY AND TYPOLOGICAL REPRESENTATIVENESS

Awareness of the effects of journal writing on the outlook and self-conception of the writer can be found in Fothergill's (1974) literary study of diaries and diary writing. He noted that the greater degree of self-awareness made possible by the writing of a journal was one of its most important effects, and that the task of keeping a journal left few persons unaffected by their self-encounter. "The diary is seldom an inert element in the life of its writer. To some degree—whether to their satisfaction or chagrin, or quite unwittingly—most diarists become what they behold in the mirrors of their own polishing" (Fothergill, 1974:65).

The diary's potential for inducing heightened self-awareness and self-understanding, and for alteration and improvement of conduct has been recognized not least of all by diarists themselves. Writers of personal documents have recognized the self-knowledge potential of this activity from sixteenth-century Puritan confessionals to the modern documents produced by women interested in exploring new definitions of self and sex role.[12] Effects and consequences of this particularly reflexive form of writing range from moral and spiritual improvement to cognizance and clarification of the self, from the goal of confession and resolution to the wish for expression and realization. One of the precursors of the modern diary was the religious confessional, a document produced with the goal of obtaining a chronicle of trials and tribulations for confession and absolvement, so that conduct could be improved in the future. The goal of confession and improvement of the soul predominated especially in the Puritan journals produced before the time of Pepys.

Expression of ideas and feelings in order to realize and come to terms with the self is a more modern goal of personal documents, but one that was manifest at least by the time of W.N.P. Barbellion's (1919) *Diary of a Disappointed Man* (Allport, 1942; Fothergill, 1974). Recently, psychologists and therapists have begun to recognize the reflective and therapeutic potential of the personal journal (Progoff, 1975). Rainer (1978:15–19) described the "new diary" as a "practical psychological tool" for increasing self-awareness, self-acceptance, personal growth, and creativity.

In the sociological literature, Bukowski (1974), described the use of personal documents by Polish sociologists, and made an argument for typological representativeness from the standpoint of the heightened self-and social consciousness of the writers. Bukowski argued that autobiographical writers were not "average" persons, but were characterized by a higher awareness of individual, social, and cultural milieus. Autobiographical documents could be used to identify typical social phenomena.

On the basis of pronouncements contained in autobiographies we can conclude on typical phenomena for determined social groups; in the life stories the young peasant generation presents not only rich personalities of the authors but also rich *common* values, common social attitudes and aspirations. Nevertheless it has to be admitted that authors of autobiographies are not "*average group* members" in the group they come from. Diarists are a *specific elite of the community which they represent*. Sociologists did and do realize this fact that diarists are somewhat different from (not to use the qualifying term "better than") their co-members of the social group. Authors of the diaries and autobiographies are characterized by a higher than average general culture, social and political consciousness, they are more sophisticated, sometimes "acquainted with penmanship," their personality is richer and their spiritual life is fuller than that of an average representative of the group which they come from (Bukowski, 1974:29).

Bukowski noted that the method of personal documents enjoyed great popularity in Poland during the prewar years, then declined, and then experienced a revival after 1956 and especially after 1961 when diary contests were instituted in which literally thousands of diaries were written and submitted for social analysis. Common to this literature was the methodological distinction between quantitative representativeness and typological representativeness. Polish sociologists recognized that collections of diaries and autobiographical documents infrequently could be regarded as statistically representative. However, personal documents could be used to identify typical attitudes and common processes of social and community life. The social researcher using personal documents discovered the typical and the common not by statistical aggregation, but by understanding the interrelationships between variables manifested in concrete individuals.

The sociologist does not expect to find in his autobiographical material, as the statistician does in reference to his material, a mass repetition of some similar facts, in order to detect in them certain steady tendencies. Autobiographers provide sociologists with material for analysis of the social behavior of the individual. Indeed, a sociologist, similarly as a statistician, is interested in a characterization of the social environment and in a knowledge of social life. However, he achieves this knowledge along a different line than a statistician does, namely, by understanding facts in their correlation (J. Chalasinski, quoted in Bukowski, 1974:28).

To recapitulate our earlier statement about the advantages of personal documents for research on social change, they are crucial both because of their content and their continuance over time.

To the historical researcher or the sociologist the personal document is above all a medium which reflects a certain historical and social process in a subjective form. It makes accessible to the researcher a look 'below the surface' of an event even far removed in time and helps more than any other source of information to capture the 'spirit of the age' ["*duch doby*"], that is to say the entire complex collection of opinions, conceptions, current of ideas and above all social relations as they were reflected in the thoughts of contemporaries (Viewegh, 1972:364).

THE CONTENT ANALYSIS OF PERSONAL DOCUMENTS

Content analysis is the name given to a set of procedures for making careful judgments about the content of communication. Holsti (1969) differentiated content analysis from any careful reading of documents in general by the characteristics of *objectivity, system,* and *generality*. Objectivity requires the formation of explicit rules and procedures. All judgments about the data must be made on the basis of definite and manifest rules. Systematic means that rules and procedures must be applied consistently, and without regard to the hypotheses of the research. Generality requires that research findings be of some theoretical significance, which usually means that some kind of comparison be made.

For purposes of this research, the definition of content analysis jointly developed by Stone and associates (Stone et al., 1966:5) is adopted. "Content analysis is any research technique for making inferences by systematically and objectively identifying specified characteristics within the text."

This definition differs from Bereleson's (1954:488–489) classic formulation ("a research technique for the objective, systematic and quantitative description of the manifest content of communication") by explicitly acknowledging the goal of inference, and by deleting the specification of manifest content.

Inference, meaning judgments about the speaker and conditions surrounding the production and reception of the communication, is thus elevated to a central purpose of content analysis. The concern with inference was one of the main areas of agreement to emerge from the 1955 Social Research Council on content analysis. The conference participants expressed "a sophisticated concern with the problems of inference from verbal material to its antecedent conditions" (Pool, 1959:2).

The latent-manifest issue concerns the level of interpretation open to the researcher, the extent to which he or she can go beyond the obvious surface meaning of the text. According to Holsti (1969) the issue can be considered in two aspects: coding and interpretation of results. Objectivity requires that coding be carried out only on manifest characteristics of the text, but the increased emphasis on inference calls for more leeway in the interpretation of results, such as going beyond the expressed intentions of the speaker (see also Markoff et al., 1974; Woodrum, 1984).

Generally speaking, content analysis designs are of three types according to their principal purpose: (1) to describe the characteristics of communications; (2) to make inferences about the antecedents of communications; and (3) to make inferences about the consequences of communications (Holsti, 1969:26). Research designs of the second and third type require additional information from sources independent of the text. The research described here is of the first type, and utilizes for the most part information gathered from the texts themselves. Although types two and three are of more importance for theory building, a theory can only take shape over against a phenomenon to be explained. Type one research designs aim at establishing phenomena to be explained.

The design of the present research involves a comparison between texts from different time periods. The same kind of comparison is made in the trend study in survey research. Trend studies in content analysis include such pioneering works as the monumental RADIR studies of political symbols in prestige newspapers, and an extensive study of inspirational best sellers between 1875 and 1955 (Schneider and Dornbusch, 1958). Trend studies are one of the most frequently occuring types of content analysis. A justification for using content analysis to study social change was forcefully argued by the authors of the RADIR studies (cf. Weber, 1983: 127–128).

There is one social phenomenon which permeates almost every social event: namely, words. No matter what change is occurring, it will be indicated in the statements of men. Whether the change is between war and peace, prosperity and depression, winter and summer, a fad for hot jazz or sweet, or between optimism and pessimism, the fact of change will be recorded in a change in the things people say.

Furthermore, a word is a sufficiently precise unit so that en masse the quantity of change in the words expressed may prove a reasonably reliable index of the quantity of social change. The words men use are the best index we have of the things on their minds. An individual in a particular situation may hide his thoughts, but it seems plausible that a change in the overall content of the thoughts of society would show up in changes in the words expressed. If so, there may be a stable way to measure the amount of change in men's thoughts, provided we can measure the amount of change in the contents of the flow of symbols (Pool et al., 1970:124).

This justification is also a rationale for using the single word or "symbol" as the content analysis recording unit.[13] Both symbol and statement analysis (the latter being the case in which the specific segment of content placed in a given category is the statement or sentence) were carried out in the RADIR studies. Based on their experience the researchers favored symbol analysis because of its simplicity.

The development of computer techniques for content analysis markedly reduced problems of reliability. Moreover, the computer made possible the analysis of co-occurrence and contingencies at a much more sophisticated level than before (Wood, 1980; 1984; Krippendorf, 1980). A set of computer programs for content analysis called the "General Inquirer" was used to study change in small groups (Dunphy, 1966), to analyze diplomatic notes (Holsti, 1966), presidential nomination acceptance speeches (Smith et al., 1966), editorial comment in prestige newspapers (Namenwirth and Brewer, 1966), and to study individual personality (Paige, 1966), suicide notes (Ogilvie et al., 1966), and self-perceived identity (McLaughlin, 1966). Since the development of the General Inquirer other computer approaches have been developed for a variety of analysis tasks (Wood, 1980; Weber, 1985). For example, in the field of applied social research QUESTER is a computerized system which performs a variety of language analysis tasks, giving companies and organizations better understanding of consumer perceptions and beliefs (Cleveland, 1985).

The design of the General Inquirer and similar studies involved a "dictionary" composed of categories that were of theoretical interest to the researcher. Each category in the dictionary was in turn operationalized into a number of single words or symbols. The computer program searched the target text for occurrences of dictionary words, and then recorded the occurrences in some manner. The coded text could then be tallied and manipulated according to the requirements of the research (Ogilvie et al., 1980).[14]

The quantitative research design of the present study follows in important respects the logic of the General Inquirer type studies, and is fully detailed in Chapter 8.

NOTES

1. See Faris (1970) for a history of the golden age of the Chicago School.

2. Blumer used the term *human documents* to refer to the letters, life-history autobiography, and other materials.

3. These would include a section of John Madge's book on tools of social science first published in 1953 (1965), and Robert Angell and Ronald Freeman's paper on documentary evidence (1953).

4. But see Allport (1942) and Madge (1965) for mention of previous resurgences.

5. An exception is Zimmerman and Wieder's (1977) "diary-interview" method.

6. A transcript of the meeting appears in the same volume with the text of Blumer's critique.

7. Indeed, recognition of this same point can be found at the beginning of Chapter 7. For a discussion of this point from the perspective of Polish research on personal documents see Adamski.

8. Information on autobiographical writing by blacks in America can be found in Butterfield (1974) and in Smith (1974); see Lawrence (1974) for a description of the 1936–1938 Federal project in which life-histories were collected from 250 ex-slaves.

9. See also Stone's (1972) paper on autobiography and American culture; for discussions of the concept of *myth* in the study of culture see Kuklick (1972) and Cawelti (1974).

10. Fothergill (1974:3) defined the personal diary as "the diary whose prime subject is the life of the writer, valued for its own sake."

11. On this point see Dilthey's (1961) comment on the disadvantages of the letter relative to biography for revealing the meaning of a life.

12. On this point see Moffat and Painter's foreword to their collection of excerpts from women's diaries (1974).

13. "The specific segment of content that is characterized by placing it in a given category" (Holsti, 1969:116).

14. An updated, applied discussion of the General Inquirer approach to content analysis can be found in Weber (1984). Brent (1984), Dennis (1984), Hong (1984), Seidel and Clark (1984), and Wood (1984) consider the use of computers for qualitative text analysis.

7

Qualitative Analysis of Personal Documents: From Resolution to Realization

The basic research question guiding the analysis of personal documents is the extent to which change over time in forms of self-concept and identity corresponds to postmodern self theoretical arguments. In order to answer this question, we have undertaken both qualitative and quantitative (content) analysis.

We regard qualitative and quantitative analysis as complementary rather than contradictory research strategies, and argue for the necessity of undertaking both types of study for an adequate understanding of the personal documents in light of postmodern self theory. Content analysis is a methodology for effecting the transformation of texts according to certain rules. Parts of a text selected for study are simplified and reduced in complexity by the transformation. The particular content analysis methodology used in this study (detailed in the following chapter) allows for a quantitative description of the word context surrounding self-referent pronouns. In a sense an associational structure of a diary is thus shown: words associated with the use of a first-person pronoun. The main advantages of such a content analysis transformation are threefold. First, the transformational rules (in a sense, rules of interpretation) are made explicit. Second, reduction of the unit of analysis to the level of individual words makes possible the comparison of texts that vary widely in style and format. Third, texts can be described and compared by means of quantitative summaries. But despite those advantages, the transformation cannot be accomplished without loss of meaning. The very advantages of content analysis are liabilities in another light: higher order meaning and intentions of the writer are lost.

The personal documents selected for study were qualitatively analyzed in order to obtain higher order meaning at the level of actors' intentions. Throughout the qualitative analysis, an attempt was made to understand the diary on its own terms, and to isolate patterns and commonalities.[1] In this chapter the results of the qualitative analysis, along with illustrative diary extracts, are presented. A description of the journals analyzed and the criteria used to select them is given in Chapter 8, which also describes the methodology used in the quantitative analysis.

OVERALL FINDINGS

The themes and ideas revealed by qualitative analysis show general support for a shift from Institution to Impulse. Especially prominent, moreover, is a shift in the way the writers thought about themselves in the context of keeping a diary, a finding consistent with the hypothesized shift from Product to Process. The nineteenth-century journals can be distinguished from the twentieth-century journals by the themes of character development and fulfillment of moral, spiritual, and secular obligation and duty; resolve and resolutions for improvement; awareness of time and human mortality; and the diary as a means for improvement of conduct and the self. The twentieth-century journals can be distinguished from the nineteenth-century journals by a search for goals; a questioning of self and others; perception and expression of feelings and inner self; and diary writing as a process of self-discovery and clarification. The themes and trends found by qualitative analysis are summarized below:

1. The nineteenth-century diaries showed more commonality as a group, and the presence of several distinctive themes. The twentieth century diaries showed more diversity as a group, and a general diffuseness or lack of specific themes.

2. The nineteenth-century diaries can be distinguished from the twentieth-century diaries, overall, by the idea of *resolution*: the writers looked upon the diary as a means to the end of individual development, and fulfillment of moral and social duty.

3. Specifically, the nineteenth-century journals contained themes of: (a) the utility of diary writing for monitoring and changing behavior; (b) almost universal acknowledgment of the writer's failure to meet social and spiritual obligations, in conjunction with an earnest desire to improve; and (c) the passage of time and the brevity of individual human life.

4. The twentieth-century diaries can be distinguished from the nineteenth-century diaries by the idea of *realization*: the writers looked upon the diary as a

forum, an opportunity for raising questions about themselves and their social surroundings, and for expressing and exploring feelings and personal meaning.

5. Specifically, the twentieth-century journals: (a) were utilized as part of a process of self-discovery, written less as a means to an end than as an end in itself; (b) were approached in a more informal manner by their writers, where the writing of the diary was considered less as an obligation, and more as an activity with its own reward; (c) contained observations of feelings, thoughts, strengths, weaknesses, and personal meanings; and (d) contained questioning and reflection on goals and values for self, social group, and the larger human community.

GENERAL CONSIDERATIONS: FORM OF EXPRESSION OF DIARY WRITING

In advance of describing substantive themes and differences between the historical groups we will give an indication of the general format and character of diary writing. We will also make some generalizations about the form of expression found in the journals.

Diary writers, especially those from the nineteenth-century, typically structure individual segments of their "book of the self" by beginning with the major outlines of the events of the day, afterwards describing their reactions and evaluations of those events. Interestingly, this format of proceeding from the objective flow of events to subjective reactions and evaluations is typical of the pattern of responses found on the Twenty Statements Test, an open-ended pencil-and-paper instrument for studying self-concept (Spitzer et al., 1973). Perhaps the single most universal theme mentioned by diary writers is the day's weather. Of course, observations about weather from another time and place are probably the least interesting topic from the point of view of a subsequent reader of a diary.

While it is not possible to give "representative" samples of journal writing, the daily entries reproduced below are typical and convey some common features of the nineteenth-century journals. The entries are reproduced in full. The first two are from the 1846 journal of a thirty-year-old Minnesota farmer, William Brown; the latter is from the journal of twenty-two-year-old Martha Hopkins Barbour in the same year.

(1) —From the Diary of William R. Brown, 1846

Thursday March 19 —Wind sprung up in the night & blew very hard from the southwest & became quite cold & snowed at times through the Day. So stormy Harrison & I did not work. I sorted out my garden seeds & put up some seeds for Wm Middleton [,] McHattie & James S. Davis Mail arrived today.

Most of Brown's diary continues in a similar vein. William Brown's journal and many like it tend to be a record of events of the day, with little space devoted to reflection about more personal matters. However, even a more "log" type journal such as Brown's does contain occasional personal reactions. The following entry is from January of the same year and tells of Brown's trip to a wedding party.

(2) —From the Diary of William R. Brown, 1846

Thursday 15th —Our Horse was among the missing consequently Martha cannot go to the Weding I promised Crosby I would take his Churn over to McHattie's place in the Jumper, but as the horse was gone I can't take it. Harrison & I went over to the Weding on Foot. Had a very pleasant time. They had Liquor & drank of which I disapproved. We indulged in the simple plays usually played on such occasions I hope the day is not far distant when such things will not be countenanced by the better sort of people. We started home at 2 oclock at night. I saw Mrs Andy McCay [Mackey] for the first time I think her a good Woman

(3) —From the Journal of Martha Isabella Hopkins Barbour, 1846

August 20th —Rose at 7 o'clock this morning and was glad to see it cloudy for the sun has been so very warm for some days. Then to have it obscured was certainly a relief. The steamer "James L. Day" came in today from Lanacca. It was a great disappointment to me when I heard she was not from Point Isabel. Mrs Johnston and Sid left this afternoon. How I miss them. I really feel attached to them both. She should feel grateful that she has a child to enliven and keep up her spirits in her husband's absence. If my dear little babe had lived, what comfort she would have been to me during my separation from my husband.

The twentieth-century journals constituted a more diverse group than the nineteenth-century journals, and it is for this reason that an illustrative entry is not included here. As mentioned above in the qualitative analysis summary, the twentieth-century journals were more diffuse in the sense of the discernibility of specific themes. Diaries from the nineteenth century were more distinctive and the easiest from which to isolate common themes and patterns. The twentieth-century diaries as a group yielded less distinct impressions, and it was especially difficult to isolate typical patterns for diaries from the most contemporary group of journals.

This difference in the discernibility or manifestness of meaning patterns between the historical groups was not anticipated and hence was not formally provided for in the methodology of the study. We should observe moreover that this difference may possibly be related to the fact that the study sample included more nineteenth-century than twentieth-century documents. However, a difference over time in the clarity, delineation, and definity of expression of themes about the self does correspond with one of the major dimensions of postmodern self theory: a shift from Product to Process in experience and definition of self.

NINETEENTH-CENTURY DIARIES

Resolution is a theme which occurs in most of the nineteenth-century diaries. The nineteenth-century diarists were preoccupied with evaluating themselves in terms of religious or societal obligations and duty. They made observations of their shortcomings, chastised themselves for failure, and then made stern resolutions for the future. The diary was often thought of as a tool or instrument of leverage in this endeavor.

The theme of resolution and its relationship to the ninteenth-century diary can be introduced by quoting a famous member of a family with a long tradition of serious diary writing, John Quincy Adams. Adams wrote in 1827:

A Diary is the Time Piece of Life, and will never fail of keeping Time, or of getting out of order with it. A Diary if honestly kept is one of the best preservatives of Morals. A man who commits to paper from day to day the employment of his time, the places he frequents, the persons with whom he converses, the actions with which he is occupied, will have a perpetual guard over himself. His Record is a second Conscience (Adams, 1964a:xv).

Adams' short statement contains nearly all of the themes found to be characteristic of nineteenth-century diaries: a concern with time and with fulfilling one's duty and obligations in the face of the brevity of human life, moral improvement, and the diary as an instrument to achieve self-improvement.

The following diary excerpts illustrate to varying degrees those characteristic themes. The first excerpt (4) is Jacob Rhett Motte's dedication to his diary which he wrote near the end of his junior year at Harvard in 1831. Motte was twenty years old at the time and "not untypical of his generation," according to the editor of his diary (Motte, 1940:vii). Motte noted his previous failure to keep a diary, but firmly resolved once more to accomplish the task, "being fully sensible of the advantages of such a plan." The second excerpt (5) is from Motte's diary two months later, and focuses also on resolution and fulfillment of duty.

(4) —From the Diary of Jacob Rhett Motte, 1831

1st May. Sunday —I have at last commenced a journal of my actions, studies and thoughts. In consequence of my having a great share of irresolution, it has been deferred till this late period of my College course; but as every one at the commencement of any new era, such as year, month or week, generally forms to himself new plans for the regulation of his conduct, and uses greater exertions to put into operation any new resolution; thus it is that I have been enabled to put into execution at the beginning of this month a resolution formed many years ago, but delay'd through irresolution or laziness. Being fully sensible of the advantages to be derived now, and pleasure hereafter, from pursuing such a plan, and being favored by the day on which this month begins, I have actually taken pen in hand, with the firm and full determination not to let the present moment slip away unprofitably and unemployed.

(5) —From the Diary of Jacob Rhett Motte, 1831

1st July Friday —Here begins another month, and according to custom, I shall review my past conduct and see with what success I have acted according to my last month's resolutions. As respects the first resolution, about missing prayers and recitations, I have been very firm, not having missed more than one prayer and one recitation since it was made. As to the others, I found it impossible to stick to them. Is it worthwhile to make any new ones? No; not until I can keep those already made. However, this term is almost out, and with a new year and a new term there's no knowing what one may do. Today wrote a forensic,—question was, "Whether genius be an innate and irresistible propensity to some particular pursuit, or merely general superiority owing to accidental circumstances?" I was on the negative side. After supper Crafts and myself walked through the Port in company with many others, who follow'd the Harvard Washington Corps in their march down to that place and back again; a march to them equal to that of the City Guards to Philadelphia.

Excerpts (6) and (7) are taken from the diary of Abner Morse, a forty-year-old Vermont migrant who came to River Falls, Wisconsin, in 1856. Duty and resolution are again emphasized, but Morse's diary illustrates especially well the goal-oriented, diary-as-means attitude that many of the nineteenth-century diary writers took toward their journals.

(6) —From the Diary of Abner Morse, 1859

[Sunday, June 5] —It has been a busy time with us for several days past, and in the bustle and hurry I have neglected this journal—a thing which I regret. I love to refer to it, but it gives me far more pleasure to see that the dates keep tally with the days of the week. While I sit and write I have a sweet season of reflection, and I know that no day should be allowed to pass over my head without I profit by such a season. It smooths the rugged pathway of life; it softens asperities, and refines the feelings; it gives tone and grace to our actions, and consequently it enhances our pleasures. The mind, or rather the Soul is elevated, and it is a season of prayer to one who daily habituates himself to it. But we are prone to neglect well known duties, and there is scarcely anyone who cannot adopt the sentiment expressed in the couplet—

> I know the right, and I approve it too;
> I know the wrong, and yet the wrong pursue.

The week that has passed has been an uncommon one for the season. Heavy rains fell early in the week, and hard frost brought [up] the rear on Friday & Saturday nights.

Morse emphasizes several sources of benefit he receives from keeping a journal. First mentioned is the pleasure received from the sheer activity of keeping the journal on a regular basis. He enjoys constructing a comprehensive record that can be referred to, and sees the journal as a product of labor of which he can be justifiably proud. Second, Morse notes the pleasure he receives from a "sweet season of reflection," contemplation about his life and surroundings in a context of self-improvement. He enjoys private reflection, but only insofar as it is carried out as a means to an end—self-improvement and fulfillment of duty.

The following excerpt, written by Morse only one week later, shows him judging already that he has neglected his duty. Such a confession about falling short in one's duty and obligations was a common theme among the nineteenth-century diaries.

(7) —From the Diary of Abner Morse, 1859

Sunday June 12, 1859 —The weeks are passing away rapidly, and I am omitting an important duty; but I have caught myself in this predicament so often that I am not now going to write a sermon upon the sin of negligence, lest (judging from the past), I should fall into the same error again before the week is passed.

The events of the week, so far as I have known them, have been nothing but those of common occurrence.

Excerpt (8) reproduces in full Orville Hickman Browning's resolutions from his diary of 1850. The forty-four-year-old Browning made an unsuccessful bid for Congress that year. The themes of resolution and acknowledgement of shortcomings are salient.

(8) —From the Diary of Orville Hickman Browning, 1850

Saturday Augt 10 —I have this day formed some resolutions which I hope by the blessing of Providence, and thro grace to be able to maintain.

There are few persons who are not guilty of a very culpable waste of time, and of a species of mental dissipation and trifling which at once enfeebles & debases the intellect, and I am conscious that there is a long list of such offences chargable to my account. I am fully aware that I have not fixed that high value upon time which it actually possesses, and I am not without compunction for its waste. I have resolved on amendment and ask the great Judge to who an account must finally be rendered, to give me grace and strength to keep my thoughts from wandering to subjects sinful and unprofitable, and to guide every act of my life into the paths of virtue and rectitude.

The next two excerpts are taken from the diary of Rutherford B. Hayes, who later became the nineteenth president of the United States (1877–1881). The first excerpt (9) was written by the nineteen-year-old Hayes during his undergraduate days in 1841. The second excerpt (10) is from 1843 when Hayes was a Harvard law student. The excerpts contain the

idea of the diary as a means to improve character and conduct, resolutions for the future, and awareness of the fleeting and unalterable
passage of time.

(9) —From the Diary of Rutherford B. Hayes, 1841

Kenyon College, June 11, 1841 —In commencing this diary I have several
objects in view, among the principal of which are improvement in composition
and amusement. From having always neglected composition, and from the
trouble which the mere mechanical execution of a piece of writing occasions me,
I find great difficulty in putting my thoughts upon paper in a clear and satis-
factory manner. . . .

By keeping a diary in which to record my thoughts, desires, and resolves, I
expect to promote stability of character. This is a quality of [in] which I am by
no means willing to acknowledge myself deficient; but if I commit to writing all
of my resolves, I shall be more careful not to make them hastily, and when they
are made I shall be anxious to keep them. In addition to these positive benefits,
I hope to derive amusement in after days from the perusal of my youthful
anticipations, broken resolves, and strange desires.

I shall not yet determine how much or how often I will write lest the next
page will contain the confession of a broken vow.

(10) —From the Diary of Rutherford B. Hayes, 1843

Cambridge, October 22, 1843 . . . What am I doing to prepare myself for the
life struggle upon which I am soon to enter? What have I learned which will
aid me in the severe conflicts through which a lawyer must pass, and by which
he is to be proved before he can reach the higher walks of his profession? What
training of the faculties have I submitted to, to give them that vigor which is
needed to grapple successfully [with] the difficulties of the most trying profession
known among men? What have I done to give me that refined and correct taste
which is required for success even in the lowest literary efforts? Alas, to all these
and a thousand similar questions which might be asked, I have but one answer.
Nothing, nothing, absolutely nothing. But it is not yet too late. From henceforth
let me bend up my best energies to the great work of fitting myself to act well
my part in the drama of life. Let not another sun set upon a day which has not
added something to my stock of instruments or my power and skill in using
them.

I belong to one law club and one debating club where questions upon miscellaneous subjects are discussed. Let me never utter a sentence in either which
has not been well weighed, and found worthy of utterance. In brief, let me in
all things work with a will, and thus may my year at Cambridge be one of joy
and usefulness.

The following excerpt (11) is from the 1851 journal of William Edmond
Curtis. Curtis was then an attorney, and later became a judge. The
journal entry was written a few days before his marriage. Here Curtis
surveys his life as a gradual progress of attaining successive roles, leading up to attainment of a permanent occupational and marital role. The

nineteenth-century writers often used their diary as a kind of platform from which to survey their past progress and chart their future course.

(11) —From the Journal of William Edmond Curtis, 1851

Saturday, Aug. 30. —This afternoon I leave for Connecticut. Tuesday I am to be married. This is the last day I pass in New York before I enter the new and sacred relation of life, to which I approach as one of the great turning points in my existence. I looked forward to college life, from that to admission to the bar, and now absorbed and wearied in the cares and duties of my profession, I look to this new existence, over which the last morning star of my life is dawning, the last in the horizon of youth, with cheerful remembrance of the sad and pleasant past.

Extract (12) is from the 1851 diary of Ellen Birdseye Wheaton. Wheaton was a thirty-five-year-old wife and mother of twelve children. Wheaton's diary illustrates the concern with religion and familial obligations frequently found in the nineteenth-century women's diaries.

(12) —From the Diary of Ellen Birdseye Wheaton, 1851

Monday Evening April 14th . . . I could not but look back on my own shortcomings in duty with a feeling of shame, that was anything but pleasant, but I trust I am determined to start with a new resolution with respect to my children. It is really & truly a noble work, to train & educate the young, and I have a large field to cultivate. But Oh! how unreasonable and captious, have I been, in my treatment of my children, what a want of moral courage—how often governed by weak & unworthy motives, and then so shamefully impatient with their little failings—I feel ashamed of myself, when I think over these things, and sorry that I have so given way to bad passions. —I do most deeply feel the want of a better disciplined mind & temper & now, at my age, & with a family around me, I have got that work to do, which should have been done by my parents in my childhood. But am I training my children any better? Ah no! I fear not—but there must be a change, may it be for the better! God grant, that if my life is spared till to-morrow, I may be enabled to keep a watch upon my tongue & temper,—and constantly to feel my responsibility, to him, in the management of my children—May it be, that my waywardness and wrongdoing, have as yet, inflicted no incurable evils on my little flock! Amen—

All the week much occupied, as usual, with little or no time for thought or reading. If I had time to be unhappy, I believe I should be so, for want of more time to myself.

A frequent occasion for self-evaluation was provided by birthdays. Many of the nineteenth-century diarists wrote at length on their birthdays, taking serious stock of themselves, especially their shortcomings. The diarists did not make sharp distinctions between secular and sacred duty but rather saw them as intertwined, such that one could not be satisfied without fulfillment of the other. Excerpt (13) is from the diary of Hezekiah Prince who in 1825 was a twenty-five-year-old New England customs inspector.

(13) —From the Diary of Hezekiah Prince, Jr., 1825

October 8th, 1825 —A very smoky day, the atmosphere so completely filled as to hide the heavens and to give the air a very gloomy appearance. Was at the wharf in the afternoon, wind northerly and cool. Called and looked over Mr. Keegan's book and found it square all to 13 cents which being against me I paid him. Paid Mr. Rice for some little iron work done for my chaise.

One more year of my pilgrimage over the rough road of human existence is ended and with this day I commence another. I have now completed my 25th year. I am getting along swiftly through the years allotted me here and even if they are many they will be gone speedily. The longest life is but a point, or rather, it is a little hyphen compounding Creation with Eternity. Year after year slips by and what is done? Do I become any more wise—and better? Have I answered any of the ends for which I was placed in this state of existence? Alas, I fear not. As for wisdom, I am unable to find her ways of pleasantness and her paths of peace. I see a thousand paths which are said to lead to them, but trace them and they will only lead you round through a quagmire and turn you out into the great common road of folly and vexation again. Propitious gales had wafted me through more than three-fourths of the past year and I had began to congratulate myself and bless kind Providence as the close of another year of uninterrupted prosperity and felicity approached; but with the month of August commenced the rising of those clouds which soon gathered and are now pouring their fury on my poor pate most unmercifully. In fact misfortune, vexation and distress have followed almost every step.

Excerpt (14) reproduces in full the journal entry of William Edmond Curtis on his twenty-eighth birthday in 1851.

(14) —From the Journal of William Edmond Curtis, 1851

Monday, Sept. 29, 1851 —I am twenty-eight years of age today. Since the last anniversary I have assumed the grave obligations of a husband and I trust that I have now buffeted the storms and the surges of youth, and that I shall henceforth safely in port, ride out tranquilly the remainder of life. I have to record besides my marriage, that I have toiled almost unremittingly at my profession the past year, and that I have secured I hope to myself, by the investment of my past labors, a modest income, which I shall endeavor to fortify and augment so as to secure a better provision for myself and mine than the precarious one of my profession.

The final birthday excerpt (15) from the nineteenth-century diaries is from Elizabeth Caldwell Duncan. Duncan was thirty-three in 1841. She grew up in New York City but made a home in Illinois after marrying Joseph Duncan, who became governor of that state in 1834. The couple had ten children together. The excerpt illustrates again the intertwining of confession and resolution in a context of duty and responsibility.

(15) —From the Diary of Elizabeth Caldwell Duncan, 1841

Wednesday 10 [March]. —This day is my Birthday & I am led to enquire why it is that I have been preserved to this time Lord forgive the sins of youth & riper years and enable me hereafter to live more to thy honor & thy glory & may my dear children be trained to love & serve the Lord grant me strength Heavenly Father to perform all my duties aright & this day would I desire to consecrate myself afresh to thee in an everlasting covenant never to be broken. Mrs. Ayers spent the afternoon with me & I took a ride in the sleigh with my Husband in the morning.

The foregoing diary excerpts illustrate the coexistence of ideas and references to religious duty with ideas and references to work, family, and other secular duty in the nineteenth-century diaries. The joining of religious and secular duty in the diaries approximates the attitude of ascetic Protestantism as described by Weber (1958, 1978). Weber (1958:80) described the Protestant conception of a calling as a "valuation of the fulfillment of duty in worldly affairs as the highest form which the moral activity of the individual could assume."

The most exemplary statements combining the Protestant ascetic and the spirit of capitalism were found in a diary of a New England businessman who was born nine years too soon (1786) to be included in the study sample. Amos Lawrence (1855:82) wrote the following at the beginning of 1828, upon completing his reckoning of accounts from the previous year. An excerpt (16) from Lawrence's diary is included because it illustrates dramatically both the ascetic capitalist spirit and joining of religious with secular duty found in a majority of the nineteenth-century diaries.

(16) —From the Diary of Amos Lawrence, 1828

1st of January, 1828 . . . The amount of property is great for a young man under forty-two years of age, who came to this town when he was twenty-one years old with no other possessions than a common country education, a sincere love for his own family, and habits of industry, economy, and sobriety. Under God, it is these same self-denying habits, and a desire I always had to please, so far as I could without sinful compliance, that I can now look back upon and see as the true ground of my success. I have many things to reproach myself with; but among them is not idling away my time, or spending money for such things as are improper. My property imposes upon me many duties, which can only be known to my Maker. May a sense of these duties be constantly impressed upon my mind; and, by a constant discharge of them, God grant me the happiness at last of hearing the joyful sound, "Well done, good and faithful servant, enter thou into the joy of thy Lord!" Amen. Amen.

TWENTIETH-CENTURY DIARIES

The twentieth-century journal writers' orientation toward self and diary writing was different from that of the nineteenth-century writers in important ways. First of all, the twentieth-century writers approached the journal less as a duty or means to an end, and more as an end in itself. They were more likely to approach diary writing informally, an activity they were free to pursue at their own discretion.

Second, there was a difference in the context and time frame of self-reflection. All of the diary writers, it can be assumed, enjoyed or perceived some benefit from self-reflection; some said as much explicitly (e.g., Abner Morse). But there was a difference in the way that reflection about the self was carried out in the journals. There was less separation of reflective comments about the self from comments about other subjects in the twentieth-century documents. The twentieth-century diarists recorded reflections about themselves in a more casual manner. The quality of being more informal and casual about expressing feelings and making observations about one's self was especially evident among the most contemporary twentieth-century diaries. Further, reflection about one's life and character in the twentieth-century journals was conducted more from a present time frame than from an overriding, birth-to-death time perspective. The long birthday entries are lacking among twentieth-century diaries. The "audit" type self-reflection in which the nineteenth-century diarist surveyed and inventoried present position against an overall plan and definite beginning and endpoint was replaced by self-reflection tied to a present context.

Third, the twentieth-century diarists who did reflect about themselves and their character did so in a different manner than the nineteenth-century writers. As opposed to the confession and resolution goals of the nineteenth-century diarists, the twentieth-century diarists are typified by the goals of *expression* and *realization*. The twentieth-century diaries contain, as the nineteenth-century ones do not, the perception by the writer of an absence of clear-cut goals or values for living. The desire for self-improvement was not lacking among the twentieth-century writers, but it was not conceived of as conformity to a standard. Rather, self-improvement called for the discovery of values and the realization of one's true self and character.

The following excerpts (17 and 18), contain explicit commentary on goals and purposes of keeping a diary. The excerpts illustrate the twentieth-century diarists' goals of expression and realization, and their more informal approach to diary writing. The twentieth-century writers were more concerned with *recording* events and *expressing* ideas and feelings as ends in themselves. The first (17) excerpt is from David E. Lilienthal's introduction to his published journals. The second (18) is from Wanda Gag's introduction to her published diaries.

(17) —From David E. Lilienthal's Introduction to His Published Journals

I began keeping a journal when I was a freshman in college. What began as an occasional record of the thoughts and experiences and gropings of a youth of 17 continued through the years: a private expression of my emotions and observations of what went on within me and around me, and of the public events of which I became a part and helped to shape.

... Why did I keep this Journal? There are, I suppose, many reasons. I kept it partly because of a desire to write as I pleased; partly to gain perspective during difficult and exhausting fights, or to indulge myself in the emotions of exultation or discouragement in the privacy of a personal journal. And in the case of a number of entries, my purpose was to think through, on paper, the evolution of ideas stimulated by particular issues I faced.

Certainly I must, from time to time, have had the notion that some day such a record would be useful to me or to others. But the Journals themselves show this idea was not a dominant one, for there are many chronological gaps and many events unrecorded which would certainly have been included if this had consciously been written for ultimate publication.

(18) —From Wanda Gag's Introduction to Her Published Diary

Thirty-one notebooks originally comprised this diary. They are full of diagrams, self-portraits and other sketches, with many crossed-out words, ink spots—even tear blots. . . .

I carried my diary around with me wherever I went, and so any time, any place, in would go another batch of "chicken scratches untidy," or a quick sketch of whatever happened to be on hand, be it a child, a leaf, or (to my victim's unfailing embarrassment) someone's feet. Often indifferent to sentence structure, neatness, and accuracy of dates, I was mainly concerned with "getting things down"—sometimes an immediate recording of an episode or conversation, or of my thoughts and emotions. Since my pen was always racing with my thoughts, the writing is scribbled and often all but illegible.

The twentieth-century diarists' quest for a realization of the true or real self, for discovery and clarification of values and goals, is illustrated by the following excerpts.

Excerpt (19) is from David E. Lilienthal's diary for 1939. Lilienthal was forty years old in 1939 and had already become a key figure in the TVA project. Lilienthal observed that religion had provided a definite answer to the riddle of life for many persons in the past, but did not hold an answer for his life.

(19) —From the Journal of David E. Lilienthal, 1939

January 10, 1939 . . . During this long, long illness, I have had a great deal of time in which to reflect; in fact, there were weeks at a time when I was able to do little else. Last night the puzzle that has been going through my head repeatedly came to a focus somewhat in this question: What is your philosophy? What is the conviction that ties everything together into a life, that integrates all the parts of your life, that keeps you going?

I don't know the answer. . . .

Ruth Benedict was a twenty-five-year-old teacher when she wrote the following in her journal for 1912. Benedict's questioning was more urgent than Lilienthal's. She spoke distressingly of the mask that she showed to the world, and of the "me" behind the mask. This distinction between a public and private self, or between various components ("mes") of the self was also made by Wanda Gag and David Kogan (following).

(20) —From the Journal of Ruth Benedict, 1912

Oct., 1912 Sunday . . . I tried, oh very hard, to believe that our own characters are the justification of it all. Bob believes it, and I think Margery would if she ever felt it mattered. But the boredom had gone too deep; I had no flicker of interest in my character. What was my character anyway? My real *me* was a creature I dared not look upon—it was terrorized by loneliness, frozen by a sense of futility, obsessed by a longing to *stop*. No one had ever heard of that Me. If they had, they would have thought it an interesting pose. The mask was tightly adjusted.

I could see no way out. All my cheerfulness, my gaiety were part and parcel of the mask—the Me remained behind. I longed to be old—sixty or seventy—when I fancied the Me might have been strangled by the long-continued tight-lacing of the mask. I only wanted my feelings dulled—I wanted to be just placidly contented when I saw the full moon hang low over the ocean. And the weary years seemed unendurable.

I am not afraid of pain, nor of sorrow. But this loneliness, this futility, this emptiness—I dare not face them.

. . . The trouble is not that we are never happy—it is that happiness is so episodical. A morning in the library, an afternoon with someone I really care about, a day in the mountains, a good-night-time with the babies can almost frighten me with happiness. But then it is gone and I cannot see what holds it all together. What is worth while? What is the purpose? What do I *want*?

Wanda Gag made a remarkably modern distinction between her social and public self "me", and her true or real, private self "myself" (cf. James, 1950; Mead, 1934). The excerpt below (21) explains the me-myself distinction, and comes from Gag's 1914 diary written while she was a twenty-one-year-old art student in St. Paul, Minneapolis.

(21) —From the Diary of Wanda Gag, 1914

April 17, Friday [1914] . . . Myself, you see, stands for my better judgement, for my permanent self, and *Me* is my unstable self, the part that is continually changing. Myself is the part of me that sees its way out of my "self-to-me" arguments, as for instance the one above about cleverness; and Me is that part that writes things in diaries in angular words, angular phrases and angular thoughts.

Like this:—Myself is inside, and *Me* is trying to sort of fit around the outside only it can't very well because it's so angular, you see, and can do no more than touch *myself* and feel that myself is there.[2]

Myself laughs, sometimes mockingly and sometimes indulgently but encouragingly withal, at my poor attempts to express Myself. I do not mind its laughing, for some day *I* hope to become one with Myself.

What in the world makes me write these things to-night? (and that, by the way, was *Me* again. Myself knows perfectly well that I can't help it.)

The chief feature of the most contemporary twentieth-century diarists was their casual yet intimate awareness of self and feelings. It did not seem to occur to them to try to sum up or reflect on the whole of their lives as did the nineteenth-century diarists.

Excerpt (22) is from the diary of a nineteen-year-old Cornell undergraduate, David S. Kogan. Kogan died of cancer in 1951, some two years after this diary entry was written. Many of Kogan's diary entries contain, as do the following, various observations and comments about himself made in a matter-of-fact, casual manner. The second extract is from Kogan's journal several months later; there he makes a similar observation as Wanda Gag about different "mes" inside his person.

(22) —From the Diary of David S. Kogan, 1948

Saturday, December 4, 1948 —Jay beat me to Helen. Dated Marilyn Davis—cute, well-built, egg-shaped head—all that one can ask—and yet I wasn't satisfied. There is still the girl of my dreams, who unfortunately does not exist at present in real life. Conversation was forced—as it usually is with females.

My relation with dates are now fixed into a pattern—I usually try to put the best foot forward on the first date—the confidence is in my own personality, and not in the relationship. And yet—as the young gentleman in Goldsmith's *She Stoops to Conquer*, I lack the necessary knowledge of when, and how, and why. Some exceptions to this have been certain blissful occasions.

Read an exceptionally good piece by columnist Grafton. It too is ONE of the things I'd like to do in my time.

(23) —From the Diary of David S. Kogan, 1949

Sunday, March 6, 1949. —Was curiously sick this eve—and tossed and tossed—full of thought on the many me's inside a certain physical frame outside called David Kogan. And thought, too, as I tried to fall asleep, of the narrow border between sleep and awake, and the difficulties of passing it, which sometimes are directly proportional to the desire to do so.

Excerpt (24) is from the emergency room diary of Theodore Isaac Rubin, M.D. Rubin was a twenty-eight-year-old resident at a California hospital when he wrote the diary in 1951. Rubin seldom wrote about events of the day without also recording his personal reactions and feelings.

(24) —From the Diary of Theodore Isaac Rubin, 1951

[no date, 1951] —Today I had a fight with Logan. It was an icy kind of undercover fight that looked like a controversial discussion on the surface. I would have liked it to break through, and frankly I'd feel better if I had yelled and really told her off. I wonder if she realized we had a fight at all. She never blew her cool. My self-effacement again (a fancy term for cowardice?). Anyway, I guess I'm still intimidated by authoritarian women, especially head nurses.

The issue: we had an overdose. There I go, sounding as calloused as Logan. Anyway, a woman came in, about thirty-five or forty years of age. Her breathing was shallow, pulse rapid and faint, blood pressure 70/30, deep reflexes and tendon jerks poor. The cop who brought her in found a bottle in her room with two 1 1/2-grain Nembutals left in it. I gave her picric asic I.M. and then slowly injected Metrazol I.V. But first I passed a Levine tube by way of her nose and pumped her stomach. It was sloppy as hell getting the tube down, and that's when Logan sounded off. She chose to tell me then and there that people had a right to kill themselves. Furthermore, she said it was darned "inconsiderate" that they chose the overdose route, which is almost never effective and just makes a lot of work for people who are trying to help people who really deserve help. Imagine this bitch deciding that depressed people ought to choose a "gun or knife" or "at least to jump out of a window—something sure." When like a jerk I asked, she was very happy to let me know that this was *exactly* what she felt and so did Dr. Madden. I should have told her off. Instead, I chose to try to rationally intellectualize her out of this lousy opinion of hers.

The final two journal excerpts are both from relatively contemporary young women. The first (25) was written by a twenty-year-old under-graduate at Barnard College in New York, 1968. The last excerpt (26) is from the anonymous diary of a young woman who died of a drug overdose some three weeks after writing the last entry in her diary. The last entry is reproduced in full here. Her age was seventeen, and the year about 1970. The excerpts illustrate the contemporary twentieth-century diarists' concern with personal experience, impressions, and emotions.

(25) —From the Journal of Tobi Gillian Sanders, 1968

25 March 1968 (Monday) —It was so easy, so terribly easy. Last night I slept for nearly 10 hours, solidly and soundly. I bet I even snored. This morning I awoke feeling beautiful as never before. The radio promised a clear and warm day.

Self-contained, self-contented, yet my self is slowly disappearing. This doesn't mean that I'm going to get me to a monastery. My creativity or whatever will still be given doses of marijuana. I shall never become the epitome of humility.

Tonight, just before now, a man named Steve Brown called. He is an architect and sculptor. His voice, even over the phone, fuzzed warm and—well, warm. We rapped about the restaurant and about Anya who gave him my number. ("Have I got a girl for you!!") She liked him; I should as well. We decided after 20 minutes to hang up so our curiosities could have some food left. No nervous stomach, no dreams about a blissful life as an architect's loving wife—just that very same peace.

(26) —From the Anonymous Diary of Young Woman, ca. 1970

September 21 —I woke up even before the alarm went off. It's only five minutes after five and I doubt that anyone else on this block is up, but I am so wide awake I can barely stand it. Frankly, I think I'm scared witless inside about going back to school but in my head I know it's going to be all right because I have Joel and my new super straight friends and they'll help me. Besides I'm much stronger than I used to be. I know I am.

I used to think I would get another diary after you are filled, or even that I would keep a diary or journal through my whole life. But now I don't really think I will. Diaries are great when you're young. In fact, you saved my sanity a hundred, thousand, million times. But I think when a person gets older she should be able to discuss her problems and thoughts with other people, instead of just with another part of herself as you have been to me. Don't you agree? I hope so, for you are my dearest friend and I shall thank you always for sharing my tears and heartaches and my struggles and strifes, and my joys and happinesses. It's all been good in its own special way, I guess.

See ya.

NOTES

1. In accordance with these goals, the qualitative analysis was not confined to the randomly selected portions of text used in the content analysis. To lessen monotonous repetition we will speak of the diaries and the diarists interchangeably, though strictly speaking we analyzed documents and not persons.

2. An illustration appears in the diary alongside the text at this point. It is a drawing of an irregular, box-like figure surrounding a circle. Inside the circle is written "my-self."

8

The Computer-Assisted
Analysis of Diaries: Self and
Social Change

The design of the quantitative component of the study will be described
in four parts: the definition of the diary for research purposes, instrument design, sampling, and coding procedures.

PERSONAL DIARIES

Empirical study of historical shifts in conceptions of self, values, and
definitions of character requires personal documents having a maximum
level of reflection and expression of personal comments and evaluations.
The *personal diary* is defined for research purposes as a diary that has as
its primary consideration a portrayal of the life and individual experience
of the diarist—as against a diary in which this concern is secondary to
the representation of events that may or may not impinge upon the
writer's own experience. The latter is the case with political and military
diaries, journals of travelers and explorers, professional author notebooks, and various types of log books or business records.

INSTRUMENT DESIGN

The heart of a content analysis consists of the categories and corresponding coding rules by which the text is transformed into a form
desired by the researcher. Stone and colleagues described coding as a
defining characteristic of content analysis (1966:17): "Considered apart
from the emphasis on research design and inference, the content analysis

process is basically the task of applying descriptors; that is, of making a particular many-to-few mapping of the text."

In a computer-assisted design where the single word or symbol constitutes the recording unit, the categories and coding rules are embodied by the *dictionary*. A first step in dictionary construction is to define the theoretical framework in terms of categories composed of symbols from the relevant language community. (The dictionary categories for the quantitative analysis are shown in Appendix A.) In addition to categories listed under the Institution-Impulse and Product-Process headings, there are several unclassified categories, such as past, present, and future time references. These forty-five categories were developed from a consideration of the concepts and themes employed by the various authors from the new self, new culture, and overdeveloped modernism perspectives. The ideas and concepts contained in the arguments were focused and delineated through an examination of categories from published content analysis coding schemes. Coding schemes utilized in the specification and differentiation of meaning included the *Harvard Third Psychosociological Dictionary* (Stone et al. 1966), Laffal's *A Concept Dictionary of English* (1973), and several coding designs for scoring the Twenty Statements Test (Spitzer, Couch, and Stratton, 1973).

A second step in dictionary construction is to specify the meaning of the categories by delineating the actual words to be searched for in the target documents. The operationalizing of content analysis categories into single words is equivalent to the specification of coding rules in designs using the sentence or the theme as the recording unit. In both cases a linkage is made between a category of theoretical interest, and the actual symbol or symbols that will be considered to indicate that category.

The complete dictionary for this study appears in Appendix A. There are 2,400 words in the dictionary. The largest category is ELO/BVS with 131 words. The smallest is Time/Future, with 4 words. Parts of speech of the same word (e.g., noun and verb forms) are not listed separately unless they are spelled differently, so that the dictionary is in effect somewhat larger. Words are categorized according to "sense" or meaning, so that it is possible for the same word to appear in more than one category. For example, argument appears in RTNAL (in the sense of a series of logical statements), and in DEV (in the sense of objection or disagreement). Most words, however, appear in only one category, and only a very few occur in more than two.

The dictionary word list was developed in a process of five operations. First, a listing of more or less common words (and their senses) was consulted and a search made of this list for all words that had a meaning similar to the general meaning of each dictionary category. The word list used was published by Kelly and Stone (1975), and describes a computer program designed to distinguish between different senses of the same word. Kelly and Stone selected a half-million (510,976) word sample from the broad spectrum of texts that had been analyzed in General Inquirer studies. All words that appeared in the sample with a total frequency of twenty or higher were selected, resulting in a subsample of 1,815 words. Together, those 1,815 words accounted for about 90 percent of the word occurrences of the larger sample. The Kelly-Stone published list is arranged in alphabetical order, with a description of the different senses of a word, and the frequency of each sense. The actual procedure used in this first operation was as follows. The entire Kelly-Stone list of words (including word senses) was read through, from beginning to end, with *one* dictionary category in mind. Words were selected that had a sense the same or about the same as the meaning of the dictionary category. The procedure was repeated for all forty-five categories, the result being a preliminary list of frequently used words classified according to appropriate dictionary category.

The second operation was to refine and add to the preliminary list of frequently used words by consulting a dictionary and thesaurus. Webster's *New Collegiate Dictionary* and Webster's *Collegiate Thesaurus* were used. Again, each dictionary category was considered separately. Words were added, and to a lesser extent deleted or transposed to a different category. Rarely occurring words, or words infrequently found in written English were not added to the list. Information on how frequently or rarely a given word could be expected to appear in written English was obtained by referring to the list published by Kucera et al. at Brown University (1967). The Brown-Kucera list is a one million word sample of present day English, compiled with computer assistance from a variety of sources including newspapers, popular magazines, Belles Lettres, government and legal documents, scientific journal articles, technical manuals, and fiction. As a rule-of-thumb, words that appeared less than ten times in the Brown-Kucera list were excluded.

The third operation was to consult Laffal's (1973) concept dictionary, which contains over 23,000 English words classified into 117 basic conceptual groupings on the basis of psychological, and not necessarily logical, meaning and relatedness. Laffal grouped words together not according to an a priori logical scheme, but according to similarity, relatedness, and association in actual usage. He described the approach as empirical and psychologically oriented, rather than a priori and logical. Again, in this operation the developing dictionary categories were added to, deleted from, or changed in order to increase the concept validity of each category and to improve its internal consistency. Many of the concepts underlying the dictionary categories used in the present study are derived largely from concepts and categories appearing in the Laffal concept dictionary.

A fourth operation was to identify additional forms of dictionary words differing from the spelling of the core form which was usually a noun or verb. This included, for example, adjective and adverb forms. The operation was accomplished by consulting the alphabetical listing of Brown-Kucera. Each dictionary word was located, and a search made of adjacent words spelled similarly. For example, near the dictionary words *vary* and *varies* were discovered the related forms *variable, variation* and *variations.*

The fifth and final dictionary construction procedure was to search the actual diary samples for unusual or archaic words, or words common to the diaries but not to modern English as reflected by the Kelly-Stone, Brown-Kucera, or Laffal lists. Included among the words added to the dictionary by this last operation were many religious references, including *meeting, prayer, heaven, sermon,* and *salvation.*

SAMPLING DOCUMENTS

Sampling in content analysis may be divided into *sampling documents* and *sampling within documents* (Holsti, 1969). The method of sampling documents used in the study will be discussed first. The postmodern self writings did not clearly indicate an exact time frame, but suggested a contrast between diaries from twentieth-century persons and those from an earlier period. After an examination of bibliographies (Freidel, 1974; U.S. Library of Congress, 1960), and collections of diary excerpts (Dunaway and Evans, 1957; Berger and Berger, 1957; Moffat and Painter, 1974), the decision was made to obtain diaries written by persons born at about the turn of the nineteenth century, and compare them with diaries written by persons born at about the turn of the twentieth century, and also with a more contemporary group of persons born later in the twentieth century.

The choice of sampling pattern reflected several considerations. First, there was to be no overlap in the lifetimes of the nineteenth-century versus the twentieth-century diarists; difference in historical time should be maximized. Second, since soldier or war diaries were not a focus, the Civil War years were bypassed. Another reason for skipping the Civil War years was that the number of diaries written (and subsequently appearing in print) increased significantly during this period, thus making sampling considerably more difficult (Barton, 1974). Third, each birth cohort was limited to about twenty-five years in order to obtain a maximum of consistency in the historical experience of persons involved. It was also necessary to narrow the search in order to have a realistic possibility of covering the field adequately.

The actual years used as cutting points for the birth cohorts were approximately 1795–1820 (males), 1805–1830 (females), 1880–1905, and

1930-present. This pattern reflected the relative concentrations of published diaries in those years revealed by the initial bibliographic search. The slight difference between males and females in the earlier group was designed to include a maximum of each sex, based on the number of published diaries initially located for those years. In addition, these groupings had the effect of separating the generations of diarists by about a century.

Again, in order to narrow the field and to maximize consistency over time of an individual diary, documents written by persons from about age twenty to age forty were targeted. This meant that the study included diaries written approximately between 1815 and 1860, 1900 and 1945, and after 1950. A summary of the sampling criteria, in order of priority, is listed below.

Summary of Sampling Criteria

1. The diary writer was born during one of three time periods: 1795–1820 (males), 1805–1830 (females), 1880–1905, and 1930-present.

2. The published portion of the diary was written while its writer was between the ages of twenty and forty, that is, during one of the periods: ca. 1815–1860, 1900–1945, and 1950-present.

3. The text conformed in most respects to the definition of the personal diary given above. Specifically, travel, gold-rush, Civil War, professional writer, and clergy diaries and journals were excluded. Ideally the diary was written in a familiar and preferably a home setting.

4. Editing was minimal. Editorial deletions were indicated, and were made ideally only on grounds of an illegible manuscript.

5. The diary was not meant expressly for publication.

6. The diarist was preferably a native born U.S. citizen.

The actual search for diary titles was far-flung and ranged from serial bibliographies, to books, to the *National Union Catalog*.

The preliminary search of three diary excerpt collections (Berger and Berger, 1957; Dunaway and Evans, 1957; Moffat and Painter, 1974), and the two historical bibliographies (U.S. Library of Congress, 1960; Freidel, 1974) yielded a list of fifty-three titles that satisfied at least two of the first three sampling criteria. Next Matthews' (1974) bibliography of diaries in manuscript was consulted. Items identified by Matthews as private or personal were recorded. The *National Union Catalog* (U.S. Library of Congress, 1968) was searched to determine which, if any, of these diaries existed also in published form (Matthews did not indicate which particular manuscripts also existed in published form). Two hundred and seventy-eight documents were found that he identified as being private or personal diaries. Ten were located that existed in some kind of published form, and that satisfied criteria one through three. Next, the three primary sources were searched: the Modern Humanities Research Association's *Annual Bibliography of English Language and Literature* (1921), *America: History and Life* (American Bibliographical Center, 1964) and Matthews' bibliography of American diaries written prior to 1861 (1959). The *Annual Bibliography* listed some 271 published journals, letters, diaries, and memoirs. These citations unfortunately did not contain information on the dates of the document, the age or nationality of the author, or the type of diary. Citations from *America: History and Life* and from Matthews' work did contain vital background information as well as a brief statement about the content of the diary itself. These sources were used wherever possible to cross-check the *Annual Bibliography*. Of the 215 diaries, letters, and journals found in *America: History and Life*, 160 titles were noted to be personal or private.

Many of the more contemporary twentieth-century diaries were found in *The Library Journal Book Review* (R.R. Bowker, 1967), and from the diary excerpt collections already mentioned. As is often the case when working with journals and diaries—a continually expanding body of literature— one of the diaries (that of Hezekiah Prince) used in the study was discovered at a bookstore in a box of sale books; it had been listed in none of the compilations reviewed. (A listing of bibliographic sources considered but not cited in the text can be found in Appendix B.)

All of the sources together yielded a total of 750 titles. That figure was reduced according to the sampling criteria by degrees. About one-third of this total satisfied at least one of the first three criteria. One of the considerations in the final reduction was the typical length of a single entry. Diaries with typical entries containing less than forty to fifty words seldom focused on personal details but resembled more a log or record of events. As a rule of thumb diaries with a mean word per entry (calculated over the course of one year) of less than forty were dropped out of the sample.

A total of thirty-two diaries were selected for study. The diary writers are listed in Table 8.1 by time period.

Social Characteristics of the Diarists

The final selection of diaries for use in the study was based primarily upon criteria relating to characteristics of the text itself and secondarily upon criteria relating to social characteristics of the writer. This emphasis seemed appropriate in view of the facts that: (1) the postmodern self arguments are addressed to cultural phenomena, values, and conceptions of self; (2) postmodern self arguments did not elaborate a research methodology; and (3) there was no previous empirical knowledge of

Table 8.1
Authors and Year(s) of Diaries Selected for Content Analysis

Time 1 (1818–1860)

Charles Francis Adams, 1829
Christopher Columbus Baldwin, 1830
William R. Brown, 1846
Orville Hickman Browning, 1850
William Edmond Curtis, 1842–1844
Sidney George Fisher, 1837–1838
Calvin Fletcher, 1821
James Hadley, 1850
Rutherford Birchard Hayes, 1843–1844
Mitchell Young Jackson, 1853–1855
Benjamin Moran, 1857
Abner Morse, 1859–1860
Jacob Rhett Motte, 1831
Giles T. Patterson, 1846–1847
Hezekiah Prince, Jr., 1825
Martha Isabella Hopkins Barbour, 1846
Laura Downs Clark, 1818
Elizabeth Caldwell Duncan, 1841–1842
Mary Chipman Lawrence, 1856–1858
Ellen Birdseye Wheaton, 1851–1853

Time 2 (1911–1939)

Felix Frankfurter, 1911
David E. Lilienthal, 1939
Charles A. Lindbergh, 1939
Ruth Benedict, 1912–1916
Wanda Gag, 1913–1914
Anne Morrow Lindbergh, 1935

Time 3 (1949–1972)

Arthur H. Bremer, 1972
David S. Kogan, 1949
Theodore Isaac Rubin, 1951
Anonymous, ca. 1970
Joan Frances Bennett, 1968
Tobi Gillian Sanders, 1968

how sensitive the methodology would be to subjective phenomena, that is, a diarist's ideas and statements about his or her self and social group, expressions of values and attitudes, and comments on life activities.

Table 8.2 shows background and social characteristics of the diary authors. It presents the composition of the study sample with respect to historical time period, sex, age, marital status, education, and occupational level of the head of household in which the diarist lived.[1]

The sample (N = 32) included a majority (N = 20) of diaries written in the nineteenth century. The two twentieth-century groups had equal numbers of diaries (N = 6). Male writers outnumbered female writers twenty-one to eleven. There were an equal number of persons who were married and persons who were not married at the time they wrote the diary portion selected for study (16 + 16). The 25–44 (N = 18) age group slightly outnumbered the 17–23 (N = 14) age group.

Most of the diarists (N = 19) had attended school at the college or professional level. However, nine had not attended school beyond a secondary level, and two had not attended school beyond the primary level. For occupational rankings, Hollingshead and Redlich's (1958) Index of Social Position (ISP) was used.[2]

A majority of household heads (N = 18) were of professional occupations (ISP level 1), including nine lawyers, two medical doctors, two university professors, an army officer, a captain of a New England whaler, a professional air pilot, an instructor at a school for women, and a state governor. Five household heads were from the managerial, business, and lesser-professional group (ISP level 2), including two large farm owners who also held governmental positions, two businessmen, and a plantation owner. Three persons occupied the third highest occupational level (ISP level 3) which included semi-professionals, administrators of large concerns, and owners of small independent businesses. They were a U.S. embassy secretary, a U.S. customs inspector, and a small businessman. The remaining household heads were a janitor and an artist.

For purposes of data analysis the information on occupational level was excluded. The concentration of household heads in professional occupations coupled with the small sample size precluded the use of this variable as a control. The cases were more equally distributed with respect to education than occupation because: (1) the highest level of education attained by married women was often less than the occupational level of their husbands; and (2) information on occupation was missing on more cases than was information on education.

SAMPLING WITHIN DOCUMENTS

Following the construction of a sample of documents each document (diary) itself was sampled. This second step of sampling within docu-

Table 8.2
Background and Social Characteristics of Diary Authors

	Variable	Value	Frequency	Percent
1.	YEAR IN WHICH DIARY WAS WRITTEN	1818-1860 1911-1939 1949-1972	20 6 6 — 32	62.5 18.8 18.8 ——— 100.1
2.	SEX	Male Female	21 11 — 32	65.6 34.4 ——— 100.0
3.	AGE	17-23 25-44	14 18 — 32	43.8 56.2 ——— 100.0
4.	MARITAL STATUS	Married Not Married	16 16 — 32	50.0 50.0 ——— 100.0
5.	EDUCATION	Primary-Secondary College or Professional No Information	11 19 2 — 32	34.4 59.4 6.2 ——— 100.0

6.	OCCUPATION OF HOUSEHOLD HEAD[1]	Executives & Professionals
		Managers & Lesser
		   Professionals
		Administrative Personnel &
		   Semi-Professional
		Unskilled Workers
		Other
		No Information
			18
			
			5
			
			3
			1
			1
			4
			—
			32
				56.3
				
				15.6
				
				9.4
				3.1
				3.1
				12.5
				———
				100.0

[1]Occupational categories based on ISP. See text for full description.

ments produced a smaller and more manageable body of texts for the content analysis.

The method of sampling within documents was carried out in three basic operations: (1) selection of a year (or in some instances combination of years) to be sampled; (2) selection of "daily" entries from the selected years; and (3) final selection of actual sentences to be analyzed.

The first step was to record, for each document, the span of time encompassed by the text appearing in print. Most published diaries were found to contain entries from at least several years. Among the individual diaries selected for study, the period of time covered by the published part ranged from a low of a few months to virtually a lifetime.[3]

For each year in which the diarist wrote, the number of *entries* and the approximate number of *words per entry* and *per year* were recorded. As was the case with the number of years encompassed by the published diary, there was again significant variation in the frequency of words per entry and of the number of entries in a single year. The number of words written in a single entry varied from only a few to several hundred.[4] Most diaries contained at least one entry per week, or about forty or fifty per year.

The entries written for one year were used as the basic sampling unit. Most diarists used the calendar year as a unit of composition; they began or ended their writing in relation to yearly units of time. The year selected: (1) had the highest number of entries; (2) had the highest mean words per entry; and (3) was written at the youngest age of the diarist. These criteria were formulated with the goal of obtaining the most reflective and meaningful material, and to further increase comparability of the text samples. It was often found to be the case that the year with the most entries was not the year in which the highest mean words per entry were found. Where this occurred a selection was made between the two on the basis of the year with the greater number of total words.

The second part of sampling within documents was the selection of "daily" entries. Entries from the year selected were numbered, and then randomly sampled to produce a block of text of at least 3,000 words. That figure was suggested by other computer-assisted content analysis studies (Laffal, 1973; Stone et al., 1966). With few exceptions (Charles F. Adams, Benjamin Moran, Charles A. Lindbergh), 3,000 words represented at least 10 percent of the total number of words written for the sample year. The 3,000 word limit was expanded to 5,000 for these more lengthy diaries. In the case where 3,000 words represented more than 50 percent of the total number of words written in a year as many as three sequential years were combined to produce a larger block of text.[5]

The third step of sampling within documents was to select actual sentences to be made machine readable and analyzed. Since the postmodern self argument applies to self-concept and cultural myths of identity, a method of selection was needed that would identify statements about self and about personal values and attitudes. In accordance with this goal, all sentences containing a first person pronoun (*I, me, my, myself, mine, self, one's self*) were identified. Each sentence containing a personal pronoun was underlined as was the preceding and following sentences. This method was suggested by studies conducted by Laffal (1960, 1965, 1969; Hartsough and Laffal, 1970). In a study of the auto-biography of Daniel Paul Schreber (1955) for example, Laffal (1960) ana-lyzed the context of the key words: *sun, God, Flechsig* (Schreber's psychiatrist), and *male* and *female* references. Laffal was interested in testing competing hypotheses about the pattern of associations of these words in the thinking of Schreber, a psychotic whose autobiography had been analyzed by Freud (1958) and by Macalpine and Hunter (Schre-ber, 1955).[6]

The final sampling within documents further reduced the size of the actual texts to be studied, and produced final text samples ranging in size from 500 words to slightly over 3,000 words.

CODING

Coding of the text samples according to the categories of the content analysis dictionary was carried out in two steps: (1) an initial search identifying occurrences of dictionary words (carried out by machine); and (2) actual coding of words into categories based on the meaning of the word as used in the sentence. Prior to computer analysis the sample sentences for each diary had of course to be transformed into machine-readable form. The text samples were keypunched and then stored on a permanent file tape. Each sentence had a six-digit identification num-ber that specified: (1) the name of the diarist, (2) the number of the entry, and (3) the number of the sentence within that entry.

Identification of occurrences of dictionary words in the text samples was accomplished by a computer program called REQCON (for *request concordance*).[7]

REQCON searched the diary samples for occurrences of dictionary words, and listed any it found in alphabetical order. REQCON's output included the complete sentence in which the word occurred, so that the sense in which the word was used could be determined.

The actual matching of the text words identified by REQCON to the dictionary categories was done by four coders. Each coder was furnished with an unmarked copy of the concordance print-out, and a listing of the dictionary arranged both alphabetically and by category. Each coder received a short training session in which the task was explained and some trial coding attempted. The task was structured so that the coder proceeded alphabetically through the sentence concordance, indicating a match between a text word-sense and a dictionary word-sense by recording directly on the concordance print-out a symbol (number) identifying the category.

There were three possible response categories for every word-occurrence: (1) the text word-sense matched the dictionary word-sense; (2) the text word-sense did not match the dictionary word-sense; and (3) the meaning of the text word was unclear or ambiguous, or the coder was uncertain if a match existed.

Each text sample was coded by at least two independent coders. Agreement was obtained for a majority of coding judgments. The intercoder reliability was checked by selecting seven diaries at random from the thirty-two making up the entire sample. For the seven diaries there were 1,974 total judgments, of which agreement was obtained on 1,707. The coefficient of reliability was .86, meaning that the judges agreed on about eighty-six out of every one hundred judgments.[8]

Coding disagreements were not equally distributed across all categories but rather tended to concentrate in some categories more than others. A gross exclusion of disagreements from the rest of the analysis would have had the effect of causing troublesome categories to be underrepresented. Instead of simply excluding coding disagreements, they were resolved by coder-investigator discussion and consideration of each disagreement.[9] During these discussions an attempt was made to clarify the substance of the disagreement by considering the meaning of the text word and the meaning of the content analysis category.

Disagreements were of two basic forms: (1) positive-positive, meaning that one coder had decided on one category and the other coder had decided on another; and (2) positive-negative, meaning that one coder had decided on a category and the other had decided no category was applicable, or that the meaning of the text word was ambiguous. The vast majority of disagreements were of the positive-negative type. When, as a result of the discussion, we were satisfied that a coding disagreement should be resolved in a positive direction, then one word-occurrence was added to the category total count. If on the other hand it was agreed that the disagreement should be resolved in favor of the negative judgment, or if we failed to agree, the category count was not altered. More weight, in general, was given to the negative judgment.

Throughout this procedure, disagreements were resolved positively only in the face of clear justification. Even so, it was possible that an unconscious bias was introduced into the results since the researcher (but not the coders) was aware of whether a decision was favorable or unfavorable to the research hypothesis. To check on this possibility, the seven randomly selected diaries used to check reliability were again consulted. Of 267 coding disagreements, 66 were disputes between categories of the same general group (e.g., "debt" in an ECO/BUS sense [business], or "debt" in an RSPN/DUT sense [responsibility], both of which are Institution categories), or between unclassified categories (e.g., T/PST, T/PRES, T/FUT). No matter how resolved, those disputes would not bear on the success or failure of the general research prediction. Of the 201 disagreements that remained, 118 or 59 percent were resolved favorable to the hypothesis and 83 or 41 percent were resolved unfavorably to the hypothesis. Most of the disagreements (70 percent) were resolved in favor of the negative category.

If it is assumed that coding disagreements resolved favorable to the general postmodern self prediction should have exactly equalled those resolved unfavorable to it (i.e., 100 and 100), then eighteen decisions were resolved in error. Those eighteen errors represented only about 1 percent of the total number of coding agreements (1,707).

CONTENT ANALYSIS SCORES: OVERALL FREQUENCIES

The content analysis index scores for the entire sample of diaries are shown in Figure 8.1. Specifically, *mean* index scores are presented for each of the content analysis categories.[10] The content category FAMILY had the highest mean index score (74.5), followed by RTNAL (65.7), and SENSE (61.8). The lowest ranking categories were RESTRAIN, MOTV, and E/ANGR.[11]

The distribution of index scores over the entire sample is in part a function of various social and individual factors influencing language habits. It is also in part a function of the number of words in the content analysis categories themselves. Other things being equal, larger categories will have higher index scores than smaller categories. For this reason the distribution of mean index scores over the entire sample cannot unreservedly be considered to be an indicator of the general importance of the content categories in the language of the diarists. However, neither is the observed pattern of index scores to be taken as a perfect function of category size. Rather, a rough relationship exists between category size and mean index score.

The extent of this relationship is shown in Table 8.3, which presents a ranking of content categories by: (1) category size (number of words in the category), and (2) mean index score for the entire sample of diaries. RTNAL ranks second both in category size and in mean index score. But FAMILY, tied with E/AFFCT as the fifth largest category, has the highest ranking mean index score. Similarly, SENSE is the seventh largest category, but ranks third in mean index score. The largest discrepancy between ranks occurs with T/PRES: second to lowest number of category words but fourth highest mean index score.

Figure 8.1
Mean Index Scores of Content Variables, Entire Sample of Diaries

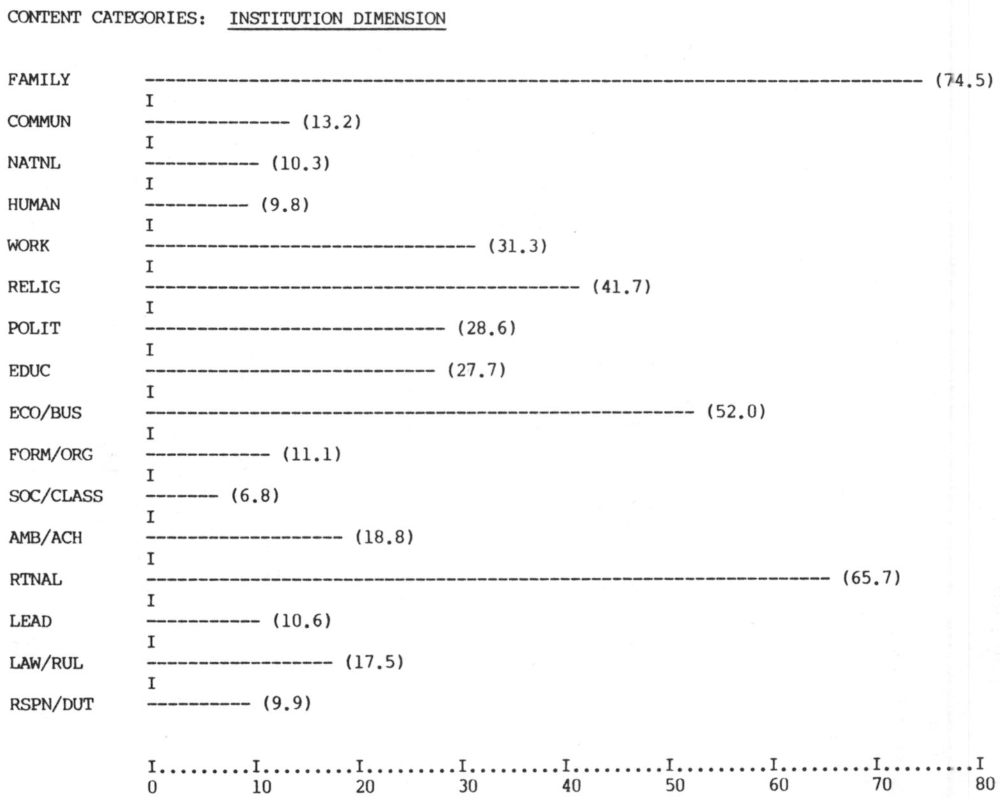

CONTENT CATEGORIES: <u>INSTITUTION DIMENSION</u>

```
FAMILY    I-------------------------------------------------- (74.5)
COMMUN    I-------- (13.2)
NATNL     I------ (10.3)
HUMAN     I----- (9.8)
WORK      I-------------------- (31.3)
RELIG     I--------------------------- (41.7)
POLIT     I------------------ (28.6)
EDUC      I----------------- (27.7)
ECO/BUS   I--------------------------------- (52.0)
FORM/ORG  I------ (11.1)
SOC/CLASS I---- (6.8)
AMB/ACH   I----------- (18.8)
RTNAL     I------------------------------------------ (65.7)
LEAD      I------ (10.6)
LAW/RUL   I----------- (17.5)
RSPN/DUT  I----- (9.9)

          I........I........I........I........I........I........I........I........I
          0       10       20       30       40       50       60       70       80
```

96

CONTENT CATEGORIES: <u>IMPULSE DIMENSION</u>

```
SENSE     --------------------------------------------------- (61.8)
          I
E/AROUS   ------------------------------------- (43.3)
          I
E/AFFCT   ----------------------------- (35.1)
          I
E/PLEAS   ------------------------------------------- (52.7)
          I
E/DSTRSS  ---------------------- (26.7)
          I
E/ANGR    --- (3.9)
          I
MOTV      -- (2.3)
          I
IRRAT     --- (4.1)
          I
EXPER     ---------- (12.6)
          I
DEV       ----------- (14.2)
          I
NATRL     ------ (7.4)
          I
NOV/SPON  ----------- (14.2)
```

CONTENT CATEGORIES: <u>PRODUCT DIMENSION</u>

```
STRUCT    ----- (5.5)
          I
EVER      ----------------------- (27.8)
          I
GOOD      ------------------------ (29.6)
          I
BAD       -------- (10.3)
          I
COMPLETE  ------------------ (23.0)
          I
INCOMP    ----- (4.8)
```

```
I........I........I........I........I........I........I........I........I
0       10       20       30       40       50       60       70       80
```

Figure 8.1 (continued)

CONTENT CATEGORIES: <u>PROCESS DIMENSION</u>

BLUR   ——— (5.8)

VARY   I——— (6.2)

MANY   I——————— (14.5)

PRCSS   I——————— (12.0)

EVNT   I——————— (13.7)

DISC   I——————————— (20.1)

CONTENT CATEGORIES: <u>UNCLASSIFIED</u>

T/PST   I——————————————————————— (44.5)

T/FUT   I——— (8.7)

T/PRES   I——————————————————————————————— (55.8)

INDIV   I——— (8.2)

RESTRAIN   I— (1.9)

```
I.........I.........I.........I.........I.........I.........I.........I.........I
0        10        20        30        40        50        60        70        80
```

Table 8.3
Ranking of Content Categories by Category Size and by Mean Index Score
(Entire Sample)

Rank		Number of Words in Category	Rank		Mean Index Score
1	ECO/BUS	(131)	1	FAMILY	(74.5)
2	RTNAL	(119)	2	RTNAL	(65.7)
3	WORK	(95)	3	SENSE	(61.8)
4	RELIG	(91)	4	T/PRES	(55.8)
5	E/AFFCT	(86)	5	E/PLEAS	(52.7)
	FAMILY	(86)	6	ECO/BUS	(52.0)
6	E/DSTRSS	(85)	7	T/PST	(44.5)
7	POLIT	(80)	8	E/AROUS	(43.3)
	SENSE	(80)	9	RELIG	(41.7)
8	E/PLEAS	(79)	10	E/AFFCT	(35.1)
9	AMB/ACH	(77)	11	WORK	(31.3)
10	GOOD	(76)	12	GOOD	(29.6)
11	E/AROUS	(73)	13	POLIT	(28.6)
12	DEV	(69)	14	EVER	(27.8)
13	EVER	(68)	15	EDUC	(27.7)
14	EVNT	(63)	16	E/DSTRSS	(26.7)
15	LEAD	(61)	17	COMPLETE	(23.0)
16	SOC/CLASS	(58)	18	DISC	(20.1)
17	DISC	(56)	19	AMB/ACH	(18.8)
18	STRUCT	(53)	20	LAW/RUL	(17.5)
19	EDUC	(52)	21	MANY	(14.5)
	EXPER	(52)	22	DEV	(14.2)
20	RSPN/DUT	(50)		NOV/SPON	(14.2)
21	LAW/RUL	(49)	23	EVNT	(13.7)
22	COMPLETE	(48)	24	COMMUN	(13.2)
23	RESTRAIN	(47)	25	EXPER	(12.6)
24	BAD	(43)	26	PRCSS	(12.0)
	E/ANGR	(43)	27	FORM/ORG	(11.1)
25	NATNL	(42)	28	LEAD	(10.6)
26	T/PST	(41)	29	NATNL	(10.3)
27	VARY	(37)		BAD	(10.3)
	IRRAT	(37)	30	RSPN/DUT	(9.9)
28	PRCSS	(36)	31	HUMAN	(9.8)
29	NOV/SPON	(34)	32	T/FUT	(8.7)
30	MANY	(33)	33	INDIV	(8.2)
31	NATRL	(30)	34	NATRL	(7.4)
	COMMUN	(30)	35	SOC/CLASS	(6.8)
32	FORM/ORG	(29)	36	VARY	(6.2)
33	BLUR	(28)	37	BLUR	(5.8)
	INCOMP	(28)	38	STRUCT	(5.5)
34	MOTV	(25)	39	INCOMP	(4.8)
35	INDIV	(17)	40	IRRAT	(4.1)
36	HUMAN	(15)	41	E/ANGR	(3.9)
37	T/PRES	(6)	42	MOTV	(2.3)
38	T/FUT	(4)	43	RESTRAIN	(1.9)

1. Educational level was defined as the highest level at which the journal writer attended school.

2. Of the two most widely used measures of socioeconomic status, the ISP rather than Duncan's Socioeconomic Index was used in order to differentiate between the large number of professional household heads in the sample (Miller, 1977).

3. Jacob Rhett Motte's student diary spanned only the five-month period between May and September 1831. But the diary of Charles Francis Adams stretched from 1820, when he was only fourteen, to 1880.

4. Christopher C. Baldwin's diary contained one of the shortest entries for a day, three words: "Cold. Study law."—January 21, 1830. At the opposite end of the continuum, Giles Patterson wrote on the *average* 411 words per entry in 1846, and Felix Frankfurter in 1911 averaged over 480 words per entry.

5. Ruth Benedict's journal was the one exception to this rule. It was necessary to combine five years in her case due to the low number of entries for a single year.

6. Macalpine and Hunter's analysis was published along with their translation of Schreber's autobiography.

7. REQCON is one of the text-processing programs maintained by the Linguistics Research Center at the University of Texas at Austin, in conjunction with the Computation Center. Hewitt (1976) describes REQCON for the interested humanities or social science researcher. A more recent discussion of available key-word-in-context programs can be found in Weber (1985:79–80).

8. The formula for calculating the coefficient of reliability was obtained from Holsti (1969): $C.R. = 2m/n1 + n2$, where m is the number of coding decisions agreed upon by two judges, and n1 and n2 refer to the number of coding decisions made by judge 1 and judge 2, respectively.

9. We were able to obtain a reconsideration from both judges for about one-third of the diaries in question.

10. Index scores were derived from raw frequencies by first summing the total frequencies over all categories, then dividing each individual category count by this sum, and finally multiplying this proportion by a constant (1000). This procedure was performed on each diary individually (see Wood, 1978).

11. A summary table (9.6) of the meaning of each category can be found at the end of Chapter 9.

9

Quantitative Analysis of
Personal Documents:
Institution vs. Impulse/Product
vs. Process

DATA ANALYSIS PROCEDURE

The quantitative analysis is designed to be sensitive to changes in the language diary writers use when making self-references. The basic comparison of interest is between diaries written at different time periods. However, there are background differences among the diary writers (e.g., age, sex), and these differences can be expected to influence to some unknown extent the content of diary writing about the self apart from the influence of historical time. We use analysis of variance in an attempt to adjust for the differences in background factors between the three groups.

The basic data analysis statistical procedure was a two-way Analysis of Variance (ANOVA), with Multiple Classification Analysis (MCA). Each content category index score was considered as dependent, and time period (nominal scale) considered as independent. Control factors, including sex, age, marital status, and education, were introduced singly. Hence, for each content category there were actually four separate two-way ANOVAs performed: (content variable by) time and sex, time and age, time and marital status, and time and education.

Table 9.1 summarizes ANOVA and MCA results for the content variable FAMILY (as an illustration). The format and meaning of Table 9.1 will be discussed in detail because it contains all of the kinds of information upon which the analysis of results is based. Tables similar to 9.1

were prepared for each content category (forty-five in all). Considering the table from top to bottom, there are four sections, each containing different information. The top portion of the table shows the grand mean index score (74.47) of the content variable FAMILY for the entire sample of diaries. The effects of time, unadjusted for controls, are shown as deviations from the grand mean. The mean FAMILY index score for Time 1 (1818–1860) was 6.83 points above the grand mean, or 81.30. The mean score for diaries from Time 2 (1911–1939) was 33.23 points below the grand mean, or 41.24. The mean score for diaries from the third time period (1949–1972) was 10.45 points above the grand mean, or 84.92. The top portion of the table also gives the eta (correlation ratio), which measures the strength of association between FAMILY mean index score and time. The value of eta is .30, indicating a moderately strong relationship between time and FAMILY.

Immediately below the top section of the table are the adjusted effects of time on FAMILY, which take into consideration the influence of the control factors (sex, age, marital status, education). The adjusted effects are also represented as deviations from the grand mean.

The adjusted deviations show the effects of time when the effects of one of the control variables are taken into consideration. The adjusted deviations, or MCA scores, are especially useful when the researcher is trying to assess the effects of one variable upon another where the ANOVA cross-classification contains cells with unequal numbers of cases—that is to say, when independent and control factors are correlated. Since the study sample of diaries is not equally distributed with respect to time and control factors, the effects of time are not independent of the control factors. The MCA scores represent the independent effects of time, and conversely, the independent effects of the control variable. The MCA scores are not meaningful when strong statistical interaction is present.[1]

Corresponding to the eta which measures the strength of the relationship between time and FAMILY with no controls, beta (partial-correlation ratio) measures the strength of the relationship between time and FAMILY independent of the effects of one of the control factors. In a special sense the value of beta can be considered as a standardized partial regression coefficient (Nie et al., 1975). For the relationship between time and FAMILY, the table shows that the overall effect of time is stronger when sex is controlled for, as indicated by a beta of .39 versus .30. The effects (MCA scores) of time adjusted for sex effects differ in magnitude from the unadjusted effects of time, but are nevertheless in the same direction. Each of the control factors affected the relationship between time and FAMILY in a different fashion.

The effects of the control variables considered independent of time are presented in the third section of Table 9.1. Independent of time, the

Table 9.1

ANOVA and MCA Results: Content Category *FAMILY* by Time and Control Factors

Unadjusted Effects* of Time

Grand Mean		Time	N	MCA	Eta
74.47	1.	1818–1860	20	6.83	
	2.	1911–1939	6	-33.23	
	3.	1949–1972	6	10.45	.30

Effects* of Time Adjusted for Control Factor

Time	N	Sex	Age	Marital Status	Education		Average Adjusted Effect
1. 1818–1860	20	12.32	7.11	5.58	3.56	(N=18)	7.14
2. 1911–1939	6	-42.38	-31.25	-37.40	-24.50		-33.88
3. 1949–1972	6	1.31	7.55	18.79	13.81		10.36
Beta		.39	.28	.35	.24		.32
Significance of Main Effects of Time		.075	.368	.194	.505		

Effects* of Control Factors, Adjusted for Time

	Sex		Age		Marital Status		Education	
	Male (N=21)	-20.12	17-23 (N=14)	4.13	Married (N=16)	12.50	Primary-Secondary (N=11)	10.21
	Female (N=11)	38.41	25-44 (N=18)	-3.21	Not Married (N=16)	-12.50	College-Professional (N=19)	-5.91
Beta	.52		.07		.23		.14	
Significance of Main Effects of Control Factor	.004		.745		.235		.496	

*Deviations from grand mean.

effects of sex are relatively strong (beta − .52), with a better than fifty-point difference between the sexes (females higher than males). Considering the independent effects of the other control variables, diaries from younger persons (17–23) contain more FAMILY references than older persons (25–44) and diaries written by persons with a high school or elementary education contain more FAMILY references than persons who attended or graduated from an institution of higher learning.

Analysis of variance can be calculated n-ways rather than just one- or two-ways. The reason for the two-way ANOVA used in the present study is the small size of the sample and the unequal distribution of cases cross-classified on the independent and control variables. In order to obtain a summary figure, average MCA scores based on the adjusted effects of time from the four separate two-way ANOVAs were computed. This procedure does not constitute a multivariate analysis however. An average beta was derived in order to obtain a summary figure representing the strength of the relationship between time and the content category. The average effects of time on FAMILY were 7.14 (Time 1), − 33.88 (Time 2), and 10.36 (Time 3).

The significance levels of "f" from the two-way ANOVA for the main effects of time and control factors are included for descriptive purposes. This information gives an indication of what the outcome of a significance test would be if the necessary assumptions were met. They are not met by the present study.

While every effort was made to maximize the power of the data analysis by using analysis of variance, the MCA scores thus obtained were interpreted in a circumspect manner. The presentation of results in the tables, and judgments about the strength of empirical support for postmodern self theories are based on the ordinal ranking and sign of the MCA scores rather than their numerical value. Interpreting the MCA scores thus increases our confidence in the substantive interpretation of results of the content analysis in view of the sampling related data analysis limitations.

EFFECTS OF CONTROL VARIABLES ON ANALYTICAL CATEGORIES

We begin presentation of the results of the quantitative analysis by considering the relationship of background factors with content analysis scores. Postmodern self arguments do not provide an explanation of how background factors should affect journal content (e.g., how Institution type references should be related to sex or marital status). Thus, we have chosen the four control factors more on the basis of conventional sociological wisdom and on the availability of background information. It should be noted that there may be other background factors, not taken into consideration in the analysis, which could influence the pattern of results. We do find that the relationships of the control factors used in the analysis with content categories corresponds to theoretical traditions in sociology, as discussed below.

Table 9.2 summarizes the effects (positive or negative MCA score considered independent of time period) of the control variables on each of the content categories. The table locates each content category according to the effect (positive MCA score) of each control factor, and groups the content categories according to the Institution-Impulse/Product-Process dimensions. The content category FAMILY, for example, is associated with positive scores for females, persons 17–23 years of age, married persons, and individuals with less than a college education. (Table 9.6 presents summaries of the meaning of each content category. The reader can refer to that table for quick reference rather than to the complete dictionary [Appendix A].)

Considering first the relationship of sex with the content categories, many of the Institution and Impulse categories are arranged according to the content of traditional sex roles—expressive traits for women and instrumental traits for men. Diaries written by men more often than those written by women had references to work and business (WORK, ECO/BUS), politics, leaders and authority, and formal organization (POLIT, LEAD, FORM/ORG), and to rationality, ambition, and achievement (RTNAL, AMB/ACH). Diaries written by women, on the other hand, contained more references than diaries written by men to family, religion, responsibility, and duty (FAMILY, RELIG, RSPN/DUT). Women's diaries contained more references than men's diaries (with one exception) to the categories that define various kinds of emotional experience: general emotional reference or emotional arousal, affection, pleasure, distress, and anxiety (E/AROUS, E/AFFCT, E/PLEAS, E/DSTRSS). Diaries in the study sample written by men had higher index scores than diaries written by women for only one emotion category, E/ANGR (anger, hate, disgust, dislike).

The independent influence of age on index scores is consistent with a life cycle interpretation. Younger persons were more oriented toward the smaller world of home, family, and school than older persons. Older diarists were more oriented toward a larger world of work and daily events. Younger persons' (17–23) diaries contained more references than older persons' diaries to FAMILY, EDUC (teaching and education), and RTNAL (reason, judgment, and decision). The journals of older persons contained more references to WORK, ECO/BUS, SOC/CLASS (social class and inequality), POLIT, AMB/ACH, and LEAD. Younger persons were more attached to the individual world of their own experience as evidenced by the fact that their diaries contained more references than the diaries of older persons to sensory experience (SENSE), to various

Table 9.2

Summary of Adjusted Effects of Control Factors on Content Variables

Positive MCA Score	INSTITUTION Categories	IMPULSE Categories	PRODUCT Categories	PROCESS Categories	UNCLASSIFIED Categories
SEX					
Male	COMMUN FORM/ORG NATNL SOC/CLASS HUMAN AMB/ACH WORK RTNAL POLIT LEAD ECO/BUS LAW/RUL	E/ANGR IRRAT EXPER DEV NATRL	STRUCT GOOD COMPLETE INCOMP	BLUR VARY EVNT	T/PRES T/FUT RESTRAIN
Female	FAMILY RELIG EDUC RSPN/DUT	SENSE E/AROUS E/AFFCT E/PLEAS E/DSTRSS MOTV NOV/SPON	EVER BAD	MANY PRCSS DISC	T/PST INDIV
AGE					
17-23	FAMILY HUMAN EDUC RTNAL LAW/RUL	SENSE DEV E/AROUS NATRL E/AFFCT NOV/SPON E/PLEAS E/DSTRSS EXPER	EVER COMPLETE INCOMP	DISC	T/PST T/PRES INDIV RESTRAIN
25-44	COMMUN SOC/CLASS NATNL AMB/ACH WORK LEAD RELIG RSPN/DUT POLIT ECO/BUS FORM/ORG	E/ANGR MOTV IRRAT	STRUCT GOOD BAD	BLUR VARY MANY PRCSS EVNT	T/FUT

Table 9.2 (continued)

Positive MCA Score	INSTITUTION Categories	IMPULSE Categories	PRODUCT Categories	PROCESS Categories	UNCLASSIFIED Categories
MARITAL STATUS					
Not Married	HUMAN AMB/ACH POLIT RTNAL ECO/BUS LEAD FORM/ORG LAW/RUL EDUC SOC/CLASS	E/PLEAS E/DSTRSS EXPER DEV NATRL	STRUCT GOOD INCOMP	BLUR VARY MANY PRCSS EVNT	INDIV RESTRAIN
Married	FAMILY COMMUN NATNL WORK RELIG RSPN/DUT	SENSE IRRAT E/AROUS NOV/SPON E/AFFCT E/ANGR MOTV	EVER BAD COMPLETE	DISC	T/PST T/PRES T/FUT
EDUCATION					
Primary-Secondary	FAMILY AMB/ACH COMMUN RSPN/DUT NATNL HUMAN WORK RELIG ECO/BUS	SENSE E/AFFCT MOTV NOV/SPON	STRUCT EVER BAD COMPLETE INCOMP	BLUR DISC	T/PST T/PRES RESTRAIN
College-Professional	POLIT FORM/ORG EDUC SOC/CLASS RTNAL LEAD LAW/RUL	E/AROUS DEV E/PLEAS NATRL E/DSTRSS E/ANGR IRRAT EXPER	GOOD	VARY MANY PRCSS EVNT	T/FUT INDIV

107

kinds of emotional experience excepting anger (E/AROUS, E/AFFCT, E/PLEAS, E/DSTRSS), and to the general idea of experience itself (EXPER). Interestingly, the diaries of younger persons also contained more references to DEV (exceptional and unusual, conflicting and opposing) and to NOV/SPON (novel and spontaneous, easy and informal, surprised and unexpected).

The idea of selection provides a basis for interpreting the relationships of marital status with the content variables. Other things being equal, the population of unmarried persons more than that of married persons would include at a given time a higher proportion of individuals less inclined to embrace traditional values of marriage and children. The relation of marital status to the content variables is by and large consistent with this line of reasoning. The diaries of married persons contained more references than the diaries of unmarried persons to FAMILY, RELIG, and RSPN/DUT, and also to WORK. WORK includes references to career, but is a more general category which includes references to employer and employee, trade, industry, job, and pay. By contrast, diaries of unmarried persons contained more references to ECO/BUS and FORM/ORG, POLIT and SOC/CLASS, AMB/ACH, and RTNAL than diaries of married persons.

Interestingly, diaries written by married persons contained more references to MOTV than diaries written by unmarried persons. MOTV includes the ideas of sex, sexual appetite, and instinct. The arrangement of the emotion categories by marital status is also suggestive: the married had more references to emotion and emotional arousal (E/AROUS), affection (E/AFFCT), but also anger (E/ANGR). The diaries of unmarried persons contained more references to anxiety (E/DSTRSS), but also to pleasant experience (E/PLEAS).

Considering the effects of the diarists' education on content category scores, the pattern of results is generally consistent with an expectation of less traditional and more liberal ideas for persons having experience with higher education. Diaries written by persons with an elementary or secondary school education contained a greater than average number of references to FAMILY, WORK, RELIG, and RSPN/DUT. The diaries of persons with advanced education contained more references to POLIT, FORM/ORG, LAW/RUL (law and legal, rules and principles), and RTNAL. References to deviation, conflict, and different (DEV) were more likely to be found in diaries written by higher educated persons than lower educated persons.

Overall there was a tendency for the diaries of women, younger persons, married persons, and elementary–high school educated individuals to contain more references to traditional themes of family and home, community, religion, and responsibility, and to various kinds of emotional experience. By contrast, the diaries of men, older persons, the unmarried, and the college educated tended to contain more political and economic, social class, authority, rationality, ambition, and achievement references. Distinguishable patterns were less evident with Product and Process categories than with Institution and Impulse categories. An important consideration here is the fact that index scores for Product and Process categories were generally lower, and in some cases much lower than index scores for Institution and Impulse categories.

RELATIONSHIPS OF INSTITUTION-IMPULSE AND PRODUCT-PROCESS ANALYTICAL CATEGORIES WITH TIME

The general postmodern self argument is that references to Impulse and Process themes have increased in frequency and importance relative to Institution and Product themes in twentieth-century culture and self-conceptions. The relative success or failure of this argument to predict the observed pattern of content analysis results will now be considered.

General Pattern Of Results

Table 9.3 summarizes effects (average MCA scores) of time on content category index score. The content categories are arranged into six groups according to the sign and magnitude of the effect of time. For the category E/PLEAS, for example, Time 1 had the highest MCA score (6.52), indicating that the mean index score for diaries from Time 1 is more than six points above the mean index score for all of the diaries. Time 2 had an MCA score of $-.52$, and Time 3 had an MCA score of -20.71. The ordinal pattern is (Time 1) High, (Time 2) Medium, and (Time 3) Low.

Within each time-ordinal grouping, the content categories are arranged according to the value of beta (from left to right, highest beta to lowest beta). The beta measuring the relationship between E/PLEAS and time is .32.

Table 9.3 shows the basic relationship of time to each of the content categories, without regard to a category's association with the Institution or Impulse, Product or Process dimensions. The first portion of the table shows categories that decreased through time (H-M-L), or that had the highest frequency of references in diaries from Time 1 (H-L-M). The second portion of the table shows categories that increased through time (L-M-H). The third portion of the table shows categories that had the lowest frequency of references in Time 1, highest in Time 2 (L-H-M). The fourth portion of the table shows categories associated with a "medium" MCA score for Time 1, and with a "high" MCA score in either Time 2 or Time 3 (M-H-L or M-L-H).

The first section of the table shows that diary references to the cate-

Table 9.3
Effects (Average MCA Scores) of Time on Content Categories, Arranged by Ordinal Ranking (H-M-L) and Magnitude of Partial Beta

Ordinal Ranking	Variable:	E/PLEAS	GOOD	LAW/RUL	RSPN/DUT	DISC	WORK	PRCSS	COMPLETE
Decrease with Time									
(H) Time 1 (1818–1860)		6.52	4.52	4.14	1.03	2.78	7.94	1.00	1.41
(M) Time 2 (1911–1939)		-.52	-3.56	-1.70	-.32	-4.44	-8.37	-.64	-.51
(L) Time 3 (1949–1972)		-20.71	-11.04	-11.44	-3.02	-4.69	-17.48	-2.59	-4.04
Beta		.32	.30	.25	.22	.22	.18	.16	.10

	Variable:	RELIG	ECO/BUS	COMMUN	EDUC	MANY	VARY
Time 1: High, Time 2: Low							
(H) Time 1 (1818–1860)		16.70	15.89	3.20	3.21	1.06	.36
(L) Time 2 (1911–1939)		-27.93	-34.14	-9.10	-12.68	-3.77	-.82
(M) Time 3 (1949–1972)		-26.74	-17.33	-1.21	2.43	.38	-.34
Beta		.38	.34	.24	.22	.16	.07

Ordinal Ranking	Variable:	DEV	BAD	IRRAT	EVNT	E/ANGR	RESTRAIN	MOTIV	INCOMP
Increase with Time									
(L)	Time 1	-6.11	-4.53	-2.58	-2.65	-1.45	-1.06	-.95	-1.66
(M)	Time 2	6.84	-2.18	-.38	-.40	.24	1.32	1.28	2.10
(H)	Time 3	13.04	16.86	8.78	9.04	4.47	2.12	1.79	3.29
	Beta	.64	.62	.56	.54	.46	.38	.32	.30

	Variable:	NOV/SPON	EXPER	T/PST
Increase with Time				
(L)	Time 1	-1.29	-1.42	-.20
(M)	Time 2	-1.06	1.18	-.03
(H)	Time 3	5.25	3.46	.60
	Beta	.23	.22	.06

	Variable:	LEAD*	E/AROUS	E/DSTRSS	INDIV	NATNL*	NATRL	SOC/CLASS
Time 1: Low, Time 2: High								
(L)	Time 1	-4.47	-8.77	-5.76	-2.70	-3.21	-1.26	-1.60
(H)	Time 2	17.49	26.63	14.00	6.16	8.90	2.41	4.68
(M)	Time 3	-3.06	1.75	4.71	2.61	1.41	1.73	.60
	Beta	.56	.48	.48	.42	.39	.28	.27

*Strong interaction with sex.

Table 9.3 (continued)

Ordinal Ranking	Variable:	RTNAL	HUMAN	EVER**
Time 1: Low, Time 2: High				
(L)	Time 1	-5.06	-1.25	-2.32
(H)	Time 2	15.08	5.30	4.16
(M)	Time 3	1.52	-1.23	3.19
	Beta	.26	.25	.19

	Variable:	AMB/ACH	BLJR	E/AFFCT	POLIT	FORM/ORG	T/FUT
Time 2: High, Time 3: Low							
(M)	Time 1	-1.19	-.86	-3.06	-6.05	.76	.07
(H)	Time 2	14.96	3.73	12.94	30.74	4.36	1.56
(L)	Time 3	-11.07	-.94	-3.16	-10.84	-6.76	-1.74
	Beta	.51	.34	.30	.30	.24	.12

	Variable:	SENSE	T/PRES	FAMILY	STRUCT
Time 2: Low, Time 3: High					
(M)	Time 1	-7.68	2.12	7.14	-.20
(L)	Time 2	-27.26	-12.94	-33.88	-1.05
(H)	Time 3	52.00	6.02	10.36	1.73
	Beta	.60	.36	.32	.12

**Strong interaction with age.

112

Unadjusted MCA Scores, One-Way ANOVA, Interactive Relationships

Time and Sex

CONTENT CATEGORY:

	NATNL		LEAD	
	Males	Females	Males	Females
Time 1	-5.87	1.85	-7.03	-.55
Time 2	23.40	2.68	38.36	1.23
Time 3	5.96	-.40	-3.22	-.31

Time and Age

CONTENT CATEGORY:

	EVER	
	17-23	25-44
Time 1	1.10	-3.94
Time 2	20.41	2.49
Time 3	-5.84	34.86

113

gories E/PLEAS, GOOD, LAW/RUL, RSPN/DUT, DISC, WORK, PRCSS, and COMPLETE *decreased* through time. The strongest of these relationships was between E/PLEAS and time, with a beta of .32 and a greater than twenty-seven-point difference between Time 1 and Time 3. E/ PLEAS and GOOD are from different dimensions (Impulse and Product, respectively) but share a positive emotional tone. E/PLEAS includes references to pleasant and pleasure, comfort, happy and funny, pretty and nice. GOOD includes references to purity and decency, character, honor, respect, and virtue.

LAW/RUL and RSPN/DUT are both Institution categories. They complement each other: one refers to rules and one refers to following rules. LAW/RUL contains references to law and legal, rules, standards and principles; RSPN/DUT includes responsibility and duty, obligation, commitment and conformity.

WORK, an Institution category, and COMPLETE, a Product category, decreased with time. This is in the predicted direction. However, the two Process categories DISC and PRCSS decreased with time, which is not a predicted pattern. According to the postmodern logic DISC and PRCSS belong to different dimensions than COMPLETE: Process versus Product. However, a common theme implied by the three categories is development. PRCSS, in addition to ideas of movement and process, includes references to growth and becoming which are concerned with development. DISC includes discovery and finding, detect and revealing, but also seek and seeking, and search and quest, which relate to development. COMPLETE relates to the theme of development by including references to complete and completing, ending, finishing, concluding, and final.

References to church and religion (RELIG), business and financial (ECO/BUS), community and town (COMMUN), school and education (EDUC), many and multiple (MANY), varying and changing (VARY) are most frequent in diaries from Time 1 and least frequent in diaries from Time 2. All except VARY and MANY are Institution categories. The fact that the twentieth-century diaries contained fewer references to these categories than nineteenth-century diaries is consistent with the postmodern argument. VARY and MANY are Process categories, and thus show a pattern contrary to that predicted.

The second portion of Table 9.3 shows that references to deviation, conflict, and opposition (DEV), badness, sin and evil (BAD), irrational, illusion, and dreaming (IRRAT), activity and functioning (EVNT), anger, hostile, and hate (E/ANGR), restraint, control, and inhibition (RESTRAIN), appetite, instinct, sex and need (MOTV), partial and incomplete (INCOMP), spontaneous, informal, and novel (NOV/SPON), awareness and experiencing (EXPER), and past time (T/PST) all increased through time. DEV, IRRAT, E/ANGR, MOTV, NOV/SPON, and EXPER are Impulse categories. EVNT is a Process category. Categories that did not relate to time in a predicted direction include BAD and INCOMP, which are Product categories. BAD and E/ANGR, and to some extent IRRAT, have an underlying negative emotional tone. RESTRAIN and T/PST are unclassified categories.

COMPLETE and INCOMP (incomplete, stopping, interrupting and partial) are Product categories. Their inclusion in the Product dimension was based on the assumption that diaries containing more COMPLETE references would also contain more references to the category meaning the opposite of completeness. It was assumed that being concerned with the completion of tasks and events would also likely entail being concerned with the absence of completeness. Reasoning along similar lines, BAD was included along with GOOD as a Product category. The first two portions of Table 9.3 show that those speculations were not supported by the results. Diaries from Time 1 contained fewer than average number of references to BAD and INCOMP, and a greater than average number of references to GOOD and INCOMPLETE. Thus, the four categories were related to time in a consistent and understandable manner, if not in the way that was initially anticipated.

Categories that were least frequently referred to in diaries from Time 1 but most frequently referred to in diaries from Time 2 (the third portion of Table 9.3) include: LEAD (leader and authority), NATNL (nation and national), SOC/CLASS (power and social inequality), RTNAL (rational, thinking, and deciding), and HUMAN (world and humanity), which are Institution categories; E/AROUS (feeling, emotion, exciting), E/DSTRSS (anxiety and worry), and NATRL (naturally and freely) which are Impulse categories; the Product category EVER (continual, regular, and habitual); and INDIV (person, identity, and individual) which is an unclassified category. NATNL and HUMAN are categories referring to social collectivities, groups not characterized by face to face interaction. LEAD and SOC/CLASS both contain words relating to power and domination. EVER and RTNAL share an underlying theme of patterning and arrangement.

The fourth portion of Table 9.3 shows that Time 2 diaries contained the most references while Time 3 diaries contained the least for AMB/ACH (achievement, goal, and purpose), POLIT (politics and government), and FORM/ORG (formal organization), which are Institution categories, E/AFFCT (affection, love, trust) which is an Impulse Category, BLUR (confusion, obscurity, doubt), which is a Process Category, and T/FUT (future time), which is an unclassified category (future time reference). AMB/ACH includes references to ambition and achievement but also goal and object, which relate to the general idea of rationality. POLIT and FORM/ORG share the theme of institutional structure and organization.

Diaries from Time 3 contained the highest number of references to sensing and sensation (SENSE), present time (T/PRES), family and home (FAMILY), and structure and system (STRUCT) at the same time that Time 2 diaries had the least number of references to those categories. It is interesting to note that diaries from Time 3 contained the highest number of references to past time (T/PST), and the lowest number of references to future time (T/FUT).

Results Displayed According to Theories of the Postmodern Self

In order to present more clearly the number of patterns consistent and inconsistent with the general postmodern self prediction, the information from Table 9.3 is summarized and presented in Table 9.4. This table shows only the sign and not the magnitude of MCA scores for each content category. The categories are arranged by time, by dimension, and by agreement or disagreement with the postmodern self argument. A pattern consistent with the general postmodern self prediction for Institution and Product categories is: positive MCA score for Time 1, negative MCA score for Time 2 and Time 3. A pattern consistent with the postmodern self hypothesis for Impulse and Process categories is: negative MCA score for Time 1, positive MCA score for Time 2 and Time 3.

A postmodern self prediction of a gradual shift over time from Institution and Product to Impulse and Process is not well supported on an overall basis, but accounts for the behavior of some categories much better than others. The best fit between the general postmodern self prediction and the content analysis data is obtained for Impulse categories: seven out of twelve or 58 percent of the categories were in the predicted direction. The prediction rate for Institution categories drops to six out of sixteen, or 38 percent. Two out of six (33 percent) Product categories were in the predicted direction. Finally, none of the six Process categories conformed to the predicted model. Overall, fifteen out of forty or 38 percent of the categories fitted the general prediction.

Although the pattern of results conformed poorly to a model predicting a linear increase over time of references to Impulse and Process and a like decrease in references to Institution and Product categories, other interpretable patterns were evident. Some of those patterns have been commented on in the preceding discussion. In order to identify those patterns more systematically, regardless of fit with the postmodern self argument, information is drawn from Tables 9.3 and 9.4 to construct Table 9.5.

Table 9.5 presents the content analysis categories arranged by sign (positive only) and magnitude of MCA score. Each content category appears only once in the table. The content categories are arranged by columns according to whether they were associated with an MCA score that was uniquely positive for one time period, or with an MCA score that was positive for two time periods.[2] The categories are arranged by rows according to magnitude of the MCA score: each row shows the categories for which diaries from each time period had the highest number of references.

The categories associated with unique positive MCA scores for Time 1 present an interesting pattern. There are, first of all, several categories that together suggest values of traditional life: COMMUN, WORK, RELIG, and RSPN/DUT. Diaries from Time 1 did not have unique positive MCA scores for FAMILY, but column four of the table shows that Time 1 diaries did contain, along with diaries from Time 3, a higher than average number of references to FAMILY. Second, there are two categories relating to the institutional infrastructure of a capitalist society, ECO/BUS and LAW/RUL. Trade and business, and legal authority, are structural aspects of a capitalist society. FORM/ORG was a category associated with positive MCA scores for both Time 1 and Time 2 as indicated by column two of Table 9.5. Third, there are two categories that share an underlying positive emotional tone: E/PLEAS and GOOD. Fourth, there is the category COMPLETE, which includes ideas of completion, outcomes, and finishing. COMPLETE "fits" a concern with work and responsibility: task and work orientation imply a concern with finishing tasks and fulfilling obligations. Fifth, there are three categories related to each other through the common theme of development: DISC, PRCSS, and VARY. The general idea of development involves the idea of progression and movement (VARY), growth and becoming (PRCSS), the idea of seeking or of a quest (DISC), and ties in with ideas of finishing and outcomes (COMPLETE).

Considering the content categories associated with positive MCA scores for Time 2, Table 9.5 shows that Time 2 and Time 3 shared positive MCA scores for more content categories than Time 1 and Time 3 shared, or than Time 1 and Time 2 shared. In other words, the pattern of results is such that Time 2 and Time 3 are more like each other than they are like Time 1, which is a pattern consistent with the postmodern argument.

Time 2 diaries had the highest number of references, first of all, to social group categories that transcend the local level, NATNL and HUMAN; (as opposed to COMMUN). Second, Time 2 diaries contained the most references to POLIT and the highest number of references to LEAD and SOC/CLASS. Those categories contain the common element of power and the exercise of power. Third, diaries from the second time period contained the highest number of references to AMB/ACH and to RTNAL. Those categories are both concerned with instrumental and goal-directed action. Fourth, Time 2 diaries, along with diaries from Time

Table 9.4
Effects (Positive or Negative MCA Scores) of Time on Content Categories, Arranged by Time and by Agreement with Postmodern Self Prediction

INSTITUTION CATEGORIES

Pattern of Sign of MCA Scores Consistent with Postmodern Self Prediction

	COMMUN	WORK	RELIG
Time 1	+	+	+
2	−	−	−
3	−	−	−

	ECO/BUS	LAW/RUL	RSPN/DUT
Time 1	+	+	+
2	−	−	−
3	−	−	−

Pattern of Sign of MCA Scores Inconsistent with Postmodern Self Prediction

	FORM/ORG	NATNL	SOC/CLASS	RTNAL	FAMILY
Time 1	+	−	−	−	+
2	+	+	+	+	−
3	−	+	+	+	+

	EDUC	HUMAN	POLIT	AMB/ACH	LEAD
Time 1	+	−	−	−	−
2	−	+	+	+	+
3	+	−	−	−	−

IMPULSE CATEGORIES

Pattern of Sign of MCA Scores Consistent with Postmodern Self Prediction

	E/AROUS	E/DSTRSS	E/ANGR	MOTV
Time 1	−	−	−	−
2	+	+	+	+
3	+	+	+	+

	EXPER	DEV	NATRL
Time 1	−	−	−
2	+	+	+
3	+	+	+

Pattern of Sign of MCA Scores Inconsistent with Postmodern Self Prediction

	E/PLEAS	E/AFFECT	SENSE	IRRAT	NOV/SPON
Time 1	+	−	−	−	−
2	−	+	−	−	−
3	−	−	+	+	+

118

PRODUCT CATEGORIES

	GOOD	COMPLETE	EVER	INCOMP	STRUCT	BAD
Time 1	+	+	-	-	-	-
2	-	-	+	+	-	-
3	-	-	+	+	+	+

PROCESS CATEGORIES

	VARY	PRCSS	DISC	BLUR	MANY	EVNT
Time 1	+	+	+	-	+	-
2	-	-	-	+	-	-
3	-	-	-	-	+	+

TOTALS

Consistent	Inconsistent
15	25

119

Table 9.5

Content Categories, Arranged by Time and by Sign (+ Only) and Magnitude of MCA Score

	Unique Positive MCA Score	Positive Score T_1 and T_2	Positive Score T_2 and T_3	Positive Score T_1 and T_3
Highest MCA Score, Time 1	COMMUN WORK RELIG ECO/BUS LAW/RUL RSPN/DUT E/PLEAS GOOD COMPLETE VARY DISC PRCSS			EDUC MANY
Highest MCA Score, Time 2	HUMAN POLIT AMB/ACH LEAD E/AFFCT BLUR	FORM/ORG T/FUT	NATNL SOC/CLASS RTNAL E/AROUS E/DSTRSS NATRL EVER INDIV	
Highest MCA Score, Time 3	SENSE IRRAT NOV/SPON STRUCT BAD EVNT T/PST		E/ANGR MOTV EXPER DEV INCOMP RESTRAIN	FAMILY T/PRES

3, had positive MCA scores for all of the categories that related to emotional experience except pleasant and pleasure: E/AROUS, E/AFFCT, E/DSTRSS, and E/ANGR. Fifth, diaries from Time 2 and Time 3 had a positive MCA score for the category dealing with motivation, needs, and sex (MOTV), for the category containing the general idea of experience and experiencing (EXPER), for the category containing ideas of deviation, and conflict (DEV), and for the category containing ideas of escape and freedom, natural, frank and open (NATRL). Sixth, twentieth-century diaries (Time 2 and Time 3) contained higher than average references to the Product categories EVER and INCOMP. EVER encompasses the rational idea of predictability and regularity along with custom, convention, and routine. Time 2 diaries contained the highest number of references to EVER. INCOMP, as previously discussed, relates to time period in an opposite manner to its logical opposite, COMPLETE. Finally, the twentieth-century diaries contained a greater than average number of references to the unclassified category INDIV.

Diaries from Time 3 shared, with Time 2, the pattern of having positive MCA scores for NATNL, SOC/CLASS, RTNAL, E/AROUS, and E/DSTRSS, and EVER. Time 3 diaries, however, contained a very high number (unique positive MCA score) of references to sensual and sense experience (SENSE), as well as the greatest number of references to experience itself (EXPER). Diaries from the most contemporary period contained a very high number of references to spontaneous and unregulated action (NOV/SPON), as well as the greatest number of references to themes of deviance, opposition and the unusual (DEV), and non-rational action (IRRAT). Time 3 diaries also contained the most references to sex and primary motivation (MOTV). Diaries from the most contemporary period had a unique positive MCA score for BAD, negative evaluation and morally bad. Time 3 diaries contained the highest number of references to STRUCT also, another category that relates to rationality. Time 3 diaries also had unique positive MCA scores for EVNT, a generalized category dealing with action and functioning. The Time 3 diaries contained the most references to T/PST. Finally, it can be observed that Time 3 diaries contained the most references to RESTRAIN, an unclassified category. It is interesting that the most contemporary diaries also contained the greatest number of references to MOTV.

It has been pointed out that both Time 1 and Time 3 contained above average references to FAMILY, and Time 3 diaries actually contained the highest number of references to FAMILY. Time 3 diaries had the highest number of references to MANY, T/PRES, and a positive MCA score for EDUC.

Table 9.6
Content Category Summaries

Institution Categories

FAMILY: family and kin, marriage, divorce, parents and children, home and household

COMMUN: community, town, block and neighborhood

NATNL: nation and national, state, and region, people, country, population and citizen

HUMAN: humanity, folk, culture, society and world

WORK: work and working, employer and employee, professional, job and union

RELIG: religion and sacred, God, church and worship

POLIT: political and politics, election, government, Democrat and Republican

ECO/BUS: business and financial, economic, accounting and banking, owning and purchasing

FORM/ORG: organization, association, committee, conference and agency

EDUC: school and education, class, teacher, student and studying

SOC/CLASS: class and status, prestige, wealth, peasant and poverty

AMB/ACH: ambition, achievement, goal and object, drive, purpose and pursuing

RTNAL: rational and reason, choice, decision and judgment, plan, pattern, and rationale

LEAD: leader and leading, command, authority, official and manager

LAW/RUL: law, court, jail, lawyer, rules and regulations, principles and standards

RSPN/DUT: responsibility, duty and obligation, commitment, obey and obliged

Impulse Categories

SENSE: senses and sensing, eating and drinking, hearing and listening, seeing and looking, touch, taste, and smell

E/AROUS: emotion and emotional, exciting and feeling, enthusiastic, stimulating

E/AFFCT: affection, darling, friend, love, trust and warmth

E/PLEAS: pleasing, pleasant, amusing and entertaining, enjoy and enjoying

E/DSTRSS: anxiety, worry, fear and alarm, disturbed and depressed

E/ANGR: anger, annoyance, contempt, dislike, disgust, hate and hostile

MOTV: appetite, drive, need, sex and sexual

IRRAT: irrational, mad and meaningless, illusion, dreaming, mystic and mystical

EXPER: experiencing and awareness, conscious, noticing and perceiving

DEV: deviation and divergent, irregular, conflict, contrast, argue and opposition

NATRL: naturally and freely, frank, open, escaping and releasing

NOV/SPON: new and novel, informal, surprise and spontaneous

Product Categories

STRUCT: system and structure, systematic, figure, form, and order

EVER: continual and constant, regular, routine, settled and customary

GOOD: goodness, decency, correct, fair, honor, kind, honest, proper and respectable

BAD: badness, wrong, sin and evil, shame, cruel, evil, wicked and ugly

COMPLETE: completing and concluding, final, end, consequence and product

INCOMP: incomplete and partial, suspending, postponed and interrupted

Process Categories

BLUR: confusion, obscurity, doubt, puzzled and unknown

VARY: varying and changing, shifting, transitional and transience

MANY: many and multiple, mass, million, and numerous

PRCSS: process, proceeding, flowing, becoming, growing and advancing

EVNT: activity and functioning, happening, event and performance

DISC: discover and disclose, searching and exploring, seeking and finding

Unclassified Categories

T/PST: past, former, old, aged, and elder

T/FUT: future and tomorrow

T/PRES: now, present, today

INDIV: individual, identity, person and personality

RESTRAIN: restraining and confining, inhibited, confined, curbed, and subdued

NOTES

1. The primary criterion used in evaluating the strength of the interaction effect was the significance level of the interaction term from the two-way ANOVA (.01).

2. At least one of the three time periods by definition has to have a negative MCA score.

10

The Postmodern Self:
Summary and Discussion

The formulation of the postmodern self argument set out in Chapter 1 made a distinction between the structure and content of the self (lodged in Institution or Impulse) and its functioning (either a future-oriented Product or a present-oriented Process). Regarding the question of the structure of the self, new self, new culture, and overdeveloped modernism arguments described a shift: (1) from rationality and unemotional performance to emotional expression and irrationality; and (2) from institutional roles and standards, societal duty, and achievement, to individual roles and standards, duty to self, and gratification.

Regarding the question of the functioning of the self, new self, new culture, and overdeveloped modernism arguments described a shift: (1) from production, constancy, and future time, to process, transience, and present time; and (2) from a self thought of as an object built up through cumulative effort to a present-oriented self realized, discovered, and actualized in a continual process.

The postmodern self arguments were ambiguous, or in conflict about the time dimension of its emergence. Counterculture sources agreed that it was a phenomenon of the 1960s, but new self and overdeveloped modernism arguments were less definite on the question. A general interpretation integrated the three perspectives in terms of a gradual and roughly uniform shift. Postmodern self themes began to emerge in nineteenth-century romantic art and gradually became more widespread until the second half of the twentieth century when they became manifest among youth and subsequently in the larger population.

The most frequent explanation advanced for the postmodern self (as summarized in the first part of the study) was that its emergence was a reaction to the successful rationalization and secularization of Western industrial society. Accelerated social change was the second most popular explanation proposed. The other explanations included: (1) a result of the weakening (or perceived weakening) of secular and rational institutions; (2) a result of increasing importance of consumption over production values and orientations; (3) a consequence of the decline of the sense of historical continuity associated with secularization and modernization of society; (4) a result of the rapid increase or flooding of cultural images (symbolic overload); (5) a consequence of the struggle of the process life against the principle of cultural form; and (6) a product of the overdevelopment of an inherent critical movement of capitalist society.

Two empirical strategies were employed to evaluate the postmodern self arguments, qualitative analysis and quantitative analysis. As noted previously, we view these different methodologies as complementary aspects of an integral research process.

SUMMARY OF QUALITATIVE RESULTS

The nineteenth-century diaries can be characterized as containing ideas and themes which together constitute an approximation to the values and world-view of Protestant asceticism (Weber, 1958). The diaries that were analyzed from the nineteenth century showed a high valuation of work and secular duty at the same time as they showed a conception of those duties as intimately linked to moral and spiritual development and to glorification of God. Duty included school work and studies for students, domestic and familial obligations for women, and professional and work activities for men. The nineteenth-century diaries that were studied contained, second, frequent references to temperance and moderation. There was a grave distrust, if not an outright rejection, of creature comforts and sensual experience, especially such experience considered as an end in itself. The nineteenth-century diarists with almost no exceptions were singularly impressed with the brevity of human life, and acutely conscious of the passage and scarcity of time.

The first characterization of the twentieth-century journals from the qualitative analysis is that of an absence of an overriding ideology or weltanschauung comparable to the Protestant ethic. The twentieth-century writers, unlike their nineteenth-century counterparts, did not have a unifying philosophy or world-view with which to interpret their lives and the problems they encountered. The perception is of more diverse attitudes and outlooks among the twentieth-century diaries. Moreover, it was more difficult to choose diary excerpts for illustration.

The diaries written in the early decades of the twentieth century (Time 2) are characterized by their overriding analytical and rational outlook on life. By "analytical and rational outlook" is meant an attitude of looking at the world both inside and outside of self in the same manner: a cognitive and reflective consideration of means, ends, and alternatives. The diaries from Time 2 showed their writers to be keen observers not only of events and other persons but of their own personalities. Characterizing Time 2 diarists as rational does not imply a distinction between "rational" and "emotional." The word is used here in a more inclusive sense, putting more emphasis on the aspect of conscious deliberation and reflective thinking. The early twentieth-century diarists reflected about and analyzed their feelings, fears, and wishes with the same attitude they used to analyze their actions and social surroundings.

To the extent that Time 2 diarists showed a concern with self-improvement, it was a question of the realization of their true or real self rather than a question of resolution to become their better or ideal self. Diarists from the second time period saw self-improvement more as an end in itself rather than as a means to an end of personal salvation or glorification of God.

Among diaries selected for study from Time 2, there was, further, an idea completely alien to the nineteenth-century zeitgeist: inquiry into purposes and goals, questioning of the answers to the meaning of life provided by one's kin, community, and society. That questioning and doubting spirit can be seen as another manifestation of the overall rational attitude: the diarists from Time 2 wanted to choose and decide *goals* as well as means. For the nineteenth-century diarists goals were *given*, clearly identified, and largely not to be tampered with.

The overall impression given by the more contemporary journal writers (Time 3) was that they were at once more self-reflective and self-aware, and yet less so. They were more likely to express feelings and register personal observations. They did this unself-consciously for the most part. They quite naturally and informally made observations that would have been made by nineteenth-century diarists only as part of a specific occasion of confession and resolution. Among the Time 3 diarists it was taken for granted that a diary should contain comments and observations on personal feelings. Such personal reactions to the events of the day were a routine rather than special part of diary writing. Hence, an occasion such as a birthday or the beginning of a new year was not used as a platform for self-analysis. Furthermore, personal feelings and conceptions of self described by the most contemporary diarists tended to be criticisms and negative evaluations. The diary was viewed as a kind of personal forum where one could appropriately vent frustration and private disappointments. Here again, as with Time 2 diarists, there was a conception and use of the diary as an end in itself rather than as means to some other end.

SUMMARY OF QUANTITATIVE RESULTS

In terms of the quantitative analysis, Impulse categories had the best "fit" with the prediction of a uniform increase in postmodern references from the nineteenth to the twentieth century. As noted previously, the assumption of a uniform increase was made in light of ambiguity about the time dimension of the postmodern, vis-á-vis the "modern" self. The category denoting pleasant and pleasureable experience (E/PLEAS) was the only emotion category referred to more often in Time 1 diaries than in Time 2 or Time 3 diaries. All other emotional categories (E/AROUS, E/AFFCT, E/DSTRSS, E/ANGR) occurred more frequently in the twentieth-century diaries.

Institution categories related to time in a manner less consistent than did Impulse categories with a prediction of a gradual decrease. Several Institution categories *were* referred to most often in nineteenth-century diaries. They were categories containing ideas of neighborhood and community (COMMUN), work (WORK), religion and the sacred (RE-LIG), and duty and obligation (RSPN/DUT). However, references to national and nation (NATNL), political and leadership (POLIT, LEAD), rationality (RTNAL), and achievement (AMB/ACH) were referred to most often in diaries from the more contemporary time periods.

The pattern of relationships of Product categories with time was inconsistent with the gradual decrease prediction. Only two out of six Product categories had a higher number of references in Time 1 than in Time 2 or Time 3. Although theoretically that result was not as anticipated, the direction of some of those relationships between Product categories and time was substantively interpretable, that is, in terms of the meaning of the categories. Hence, BAD and INCOMP, which bear a logical opposition to GOOD and COMPLETE, related to time in an opposite manner: nineteenth-century diaries contained more references to GOOD and COMPLETE, and twentieth-century diaries contained more references to BAD and INCOMP.

Process categories had the poorest fit with a uniform increase model. The sole Process category that occurred more frequently in twentieth-century diaries was EVNT, a general action/functioning category. Again, while most of the Process categories did not relate to time as theoretically anticipated, there was a substantive logic to some of the patterns. PRCSS and DISC occurred more often in diaries from Time 1 than Times 2 and 3, and contain ideas which relate to the notion of development (becoming, seeking, finding). Time 1 diaries also contained more references than Time 2 and Time 3 diaries to completing, finishing, and outcomes (COMPLETE).

The quantitative analysis shows a shift, in general, from social role and traditional institutional categories to categories of emotion, sense experience, and spontaneous action. But as the summary of results indicates, there are some patterns that are anomalous to postmodern self predictions.

First, the twentieth-century diaries contained more references to rationality and goal-directed action, but also contained more references to emotion categories. This pattern is clearly contrary to the Institution-Impulse distinction between reason and feeling. The general form of the postmodern argument (especially that pertaining to the Institution-Impulse shift) does not distinguish between Institution roles and values from a traditional setting and those from a modern setting. For example, family and community (to use the classic gemeinschaft-gesellschaft distinction) are both gemeinschaft concepts. Nation (NATNL) and rational (RTNAL) are gesellschaft concepts. All four concepts, however, are classified as Institution categories. The data show a shift from social roles and institutions to emotion and individuality, but also indicate an ongoing process of modernization. The fact that references to rationality *and* emotion occurred more often in Time 2 and Time 3 than in Time 1 diaries implies that the postmodern shift to impulse is somehow integrally related to rationalization and modernization (cf. Zurcher, 1986, on the bureaucratizing of impulse).

Along these same lines it is interesting to note that the content categories are divided by gemeinschaft-gesellschaft as they relate to the *control factors,* but do not split according to gemeinschaft-gesellschaft as they relate to *time.* Toennies defined gemeinschaft and gesellschaft by using the concepts of "natural" versus "rational" will. For Toennies, all social relationships were created by human will. A relationship entered into as a means to some other end was a manifestation of rational will. A relationship entered into as a valuable end in itself was a manifestation of natural will (Toennies, 1957:4–5). Natural will was associated with the natural and organic, family and community, emotion and feeling. Rational will was associated with the artificial and mechanical, contract and the state, reason and the intellect. Toennies made an explicit connection between gemeinschaft, woman, youth, and common people; gesellschaft, man, old age, and educated classes (Toennies, 1957:268–269). The relationships of the content categories to the control factors do define roughly a gemeinschaft-gesellschaft split. To reiterate the earlier discussion of those relationships: there was a tendency for the diaries of women, younger persons, and less educated persons to contain more references to traditional themes of family and home, community, religion and responsibility, and to various kinds of emotional experience. In comparison, the diaries of men, older persons, and the higher educated tended to contain more political and economic, social class, rationality, and achievement and ambition references.[1]

By contrast, the relationships of the relevant content categories to time do not define a gemeinschaft-gesellschaft split. Diaries from Times 2 and 3 had more references to gesellschaft ideas of nation, social stratification, and rationality but also contained more references to emotion, feeling, and experience than diaries from Time 1. Time 1 diaries contained more references to community, work and religion, but also contained more references to law, money, and business than Time 2 and Time 3 diaries.

A second anomaly to the postmodern logic, comparing the nineteenth- to the twentieth-century journals, is the separation of the category defining references to positive emotional experience from the categories denoting general emotional reference, affection, anxiety, and anger. Time 1 diaries contained more references than Time 2 and Time 3 diaries to positive emotional experience but not to the other categories dealing with emotion. When the additional fact that the category GOOD also differentiates Time 1 from Time 2 and from Time 3 is considered, attention is drawn to a basic theme of positive valuation that differentiates nineteenth- from twentieth-century diaries.

On the basis of postmodern self arguments, an evaluative dimension was expected to be present in the nineteenth-century documents and to be largely absent form the twentienth-century texts. Rather than a general evaluative dimension, positive evaluation and emotion were distinct from negative evaluation and emotion—nineteenth-century positive, twentieth-century negative. This pattern suggests the presence of some element of disillusionment or alienation among the moderns. A complete accounting of the kind and extent of that alienation requires a more specific analysis than permitted within the confines of the present study.

EVALUATION OF THE THEORY OF THE POSTMODERN SELF

Our comparative study of personal documents entails methodological—especially sampling—limitations which we have considered in previous chapters. Our research logic is that of analytical generalization—generalizing to a theory—rather than statistical generalization. Given the limitations of our exploratory study, what inferences can be made about theories of a postmodern self?

Overall, the results of the study are consistent with the theories about a postmodern self, though they do not lend unqualified support. The qualitative and quantitative analyses indicate, from the nineteenth to the twentieth century, a lessening of concern with several key Institution values such as work, religion, and duty, and a corresponding greater concern with and awareness of Impulse themes such as emotional and sense experience, and spontaneous action. The study results do not indicate the presence of a new ideology or weltanschauung based on Impulse and Process values. The results of the qualitative and quantitative analysis of diaries show more a declining and muting of an older view of the world and conception of self, than they show the emergence of a new conception of self and culture.

In terms of anticipating the actual content themes, the overdeveloped modernism variant came closest to anticipating the actual pattern of results. The new self and new culture arguments described the impulse- and process-oriented postmodern self as a contradiction and reaction to the rational spirit of modern industrial society. Far from being a reaction to rationalization, the quantitative analysis revealed that emotional references increased *along with* the general references to rational and goal-directed thinking from the nineteenth to the twentieth century, and that both of those were inversely related to categories associated with Protestant asceticism (duty, religion, work).

The only postmodern argument that allowed for an affinity between postmodern self themes and rationality, science, empiricism and other themes characteristic of modern culture was Sorokin's account of twentieth-century overdeveloped *sensate* culture. In addition to allowing for the emergence of an Impulse self in the midst of twentieth-century scientific and secular culture where the truth of the senses reigned supreme, Sorokin also anticipated the characteristic questioning of goals engaged in by twentieth-century diarists.

However, according to Sorokin's definition of sensate culture in contradistinction to ideational culture, *ideational* and not sensate culture included rationalism and reasoning. Sorokin hearkened to the traditional dichotomy between rationalism and empiricism in making this distinction. The analysis of diaries showed on the contrary that rationality was to some extent associated with the truth of the senses.

NOTE

1. This refers to differences over the entire sample of documents.

11

Recasting the Theory: From Modern to Postmodern Self, Therapeutic Ethic, and Organizational Process

The results of the analysis of journals will be used as a point of departure for proposing a more comprehensive postmodern self theory. As part of this effort an elaboration and extension of ideas which informed our discussion of industrial society will be employed: the clash of formal and substantive rationality in social institutions and in self-concept.

FORMAL RATIONALITY, SUBSTANTIVE RATIONALITY, AND THE SPIRIT OF CAPITALISM

The core dynamic principle of our recasting of the basic postmodern self argument is based on the observation that the self-system and character structure of modern Western industrial society (the Institution-Product self in our formulation) focuses at the level of the person the contradiction between calculating rationality and substantive meaning which also characterizes the larger society and culture.[1] The "modern" self focuses at a social-psychological level a conflict and tension inherent in the larger system and in social institutions. The shift toward a postmodern self represents an attempt to redress that conflict and tension.

The immediate historical predecessor of the modern self was a self which did possess substantive rationality by virtue of the fact that it was grounded in a religious value system, in particular, Protestantism. However, religious valuational systems based on the assumption of the supernatural were undermined by the ascendance of rational calculation and the scientific way of understanding the world. The postmodern self can be seen as a charismatic movement in culture aimed at restoring substantive rationality at the phenomenological level. The movement aims at grounding self-concept and character in a valuational system which is "after modern," that is, which remains after religious valuational systems have been undermined by formal rationality and the scientific world-view; it is a value system grounded in the individual expression and experience of emotion, impulse, and feeling

This modified version of the basic postmodern self argument clarifies and expands upon the explanation of the postmodern self most often proposed (reaction to industrial society). Further, it allows for a more comprehensive understanding of the emergence and nature of the modern self, a topic which has been largely neglected in postmodern self discussions. Finally, it provides the basis for a clarification and expansion of the nature and content of the specific themes which define the postmodern self.

THE SHIFT TO A MODERN SELF

As discussed in Chapter 2, there is a tension and contradiction in the modern industrial capitalist society between the formal rationality of economic, legal, and administrative systems, and "substantive irrationality from the point of view of egalitarian, fraternal and caritative values" (Brubaker, 1984:38). An account of how this contradiction is expressed at the individual and characterological level can be found in Weber's social-psychological analysis of Western capitalist society, as distinct from his institutional analysis.

The "spirit" of capitalism, according to Weber (1958), is a construction and distillation of the results of historical investigation, that is to say, an ideal type.[2] The spirit of capitalism, exemplified with quotations from Benjamin Franklin, is a value orientation, a self-concept. In a word, it is an *ethos*. By calling the capitalist spirit an "ethos," Weber stresses its coherence, independence, and existence at the level of meaning and intentionality of actors.

The content of this ethos, though it is not unidimensional, can be depicted as representing the incorporation of formal rationality into the sphere of individual conduct, particularly the relationship and orientation of the individual toward occupation and economic life. The *summum bonum* of the capitalist ethic is "the earning of more and more money," the accumulation of which is not to be used for consumption by the individual, but saved and invested in the economic enterprise (Weber, 1958:53). Formal rationality is incorporated furthermore in that the individual is expected to exert overarching methodical control over his life and person.

It is of major importance in Weber's analysis, as well as for the present discussion, to underline the fact that this modern ethos is *irrational* considered from the standpoint of the individual's happiness and well-being. The happiness of the individual in a sensual, emotional, or existential sense is not provided for; the capitalist spirit lacks substantive rationality. Methodical self-control, strict avoidance of the expressive and sensuous elements of culture, as well as all spontaneous enjoyment of life—these are its characteristic themes and the basis of its substantive irrationality.

... [F]rom the point of view of the happiness of, or utility to, the single individual, it appears entirely transcendental and absolutely irrational. Man is dominated by the making of money, by acquisition as the ultimate purpose of his life. Economic acquisition is no longer subordinated to man as the means for the satisfaction of his material needs. This reversal of what we should call the natural relationship, so irrational from a naive point of view, is evidently as definitely a leading principle of capitalism as it is foreign to all peoples not under capitalistic influence (Weber, 1958:53).

It is important to point out in the present context that the emergence and empirical manifestation of the spirit of capitalism was *not* a product of the development or extension of rational calculation in economic, administrative, legal, or other institutional spheres. Instead, the emergence of the spirit of capitalism was brought about by developments in the realm of meaning, values, and intentionality. Specifically, Protestant religion, and especially those churches influenced by Calvin, was responsible. The ethos and self system of capitalism had its origins not in the marketplace, nor in the universal fact of avarice, but in religion.

Weber argued that the larger historic process in the development of religions was the elimination of magic from the world and substitution of the attitude that "there are no mysterious incalculable forces that come into play, but rather that one can, in principle, master all things by calculation" (Weber, 1946:139). The process of disenchantment, which began with the Hebrew prophets and developed in conjunction with Hellenistic scientific thought, repudiated all magical and other-worldly means to salvation as superstition and sin (Weber, 1958:105). This rejection received its logical conclusion in the ascetic branches of Protestantism, especially Calvinism.

Puritanism took a negative attitude toward all sensuous and emotional elements in culture and religion; it provided "a basis for a fundamental antagonism to sensuous culture of all kinds" (Weber, 1958:105). Rejecting sensuous culture, Puritanism took part in the general rejection of the world that characterized the ascetic conception of life. "The ascetic

rejects the world's empirical character of creatureliness and ethical irrationality, and rejects its ethical temptations to sensual indulgence, to
epicurean satisfaction, and to reliance upon natural joys and gifts" (Weber, 1968:280). Puritanism thus embodied a twofold attitude toward the
world composed of contradictory elements: (1) a calculating and active
orientation to the world as an empirical reality, and (2) a rejection of
sensuous and emotional aspects of culture.

The critical connection between Protestantism and worldly economic
activity occurred chiefly by means of Luther's conception of the calling
and the doctrine of predestination. Calvinist strands of Protestantism
stressed the idea of predestination and its attendant problems. Predestination is the idea that the ultimate fate of the individual—having or
not having salvation—is known by God even before the individual's
birth. Therefore, good works (or the lack of) do not alter the individual's
fate. While it might seem that such a world-view might be expected to
lift responsibility from individual believers, the precise opposite was the
case according to Weber. The psychological uncertainty of not knowing
whether one was saved or damned created an intense desire to know
with assurance, and more to the point, to have proof. Ironically, worldly
success was fixed upon as the indicator of God's favor and blessing of
salvation.

The Calvinist ethos is rational in a substantive sense despite its asceticism and rejection of the sensual and emotional side of life because
it is grounded experientially in the individual's sense of well-being and
happiness. Protestantism, like other religions, relates the believer to a
larger world of meaning and purpose which stands outside the present
one. The believer is oriented, especially, toward a vastly different time
frame. Instead of three score and ten years the individual is oriented to
a perspective of eternity and infinite time. Seen from this larger perspective the Protestant ethos is substantively rational even though in
the short run an ascetic avoidance of the spontaneous enjoyment of life
and sensual enjoyments is necessary.

Eventually the religious foundations of the Protestant ascetic world-
view were undermined. The triumph of the scientific world-view and
the success of the capitalistic system undermined the very religious
outlook that had helped them to usurp the traditional order (Weber,
1978b:169–173). The inexorable process of rationalization and modernization extended into all areas of social organization and culture, and the
reach of religion abated. The modern technological and scientific world,
keyed to the truth of the senses, was given succor and helped to fruition
by the transfer of asceticism from the monastic cell to the life of the
calling (Weber, 1978b:170). However, the ascetic spirit eventually escaped its confines, leaving behind the rational, calculating, and empirical
outlook.

THE POSTMODERN SELF AS A CHARISMATIC MOVEMENT IN MODERN CULTURE

It was realized by Weber that there would be a search for alternatives to the problems of modernity and the formal substantive rationality clash found in the modern self. Indeed, the search for meaning would intensify in the modern world because the rise of science and formal rationality insured that no single value sphere would be able to claim legitimacy.

Instead of abating, the need for meaning becomes more acute with the progress of rationalization, especially with the development of the scientific world-view and the attendant "disenchantment" of the world. Yet at the same time that it becomes more acute, the need for meaning becomes more difficult to satisfy, for the scientific "disenchantment" of the world carries with it the message of its own barrenness as a source of meaning. Science yields no value-orientations . . . (Brubaker, 1984:66).

The postmodern self can be seen as part of a charismatic reaction to the contradiction between formal and substantive rationality embodied in the modern self. Weber's concept of charisma can be usefully extended and interpreted to be part of the normal process of social change and institution building (Eisenstadt, 1968; 1973). Such an interpretation of charisma puts less stress on an institution versus charisma dichotomy and instead emphasizes the dual tendencies of the charismatic, a potential for both the destruction and the innovation of institutions.

The basis of the appeal of the charismatic can be found in the search for meaning engaged in by all human beings, both individually and collectively: "[the] charismatic fervor is rooted in the attempt to come into contact with the very essence of being, to go to the very roots of existence, of cosmic, social, and cultural order, to what is seen as sacred and fundamental" (Eisenstadt, 1968:xix). The charismatic leader or movement appeals to us because of its penetration of the everyday and the mundane and its contact with some central feature of human existence (Eisenstadt, 1968:xxvi-xxxii; 1973:124–129; Shils, 1965).

The charismatic penetrates beyond existing social relations and institutions but it also can become the basis for new social orders. The extraordinary and rule-breaking charismatic can become codified and subject to rules. The process of routinization is the transformation of the charismatic as institution destroyer to the charismatic as institution builder. It reflects the operation of what Zurcher (1967) has referred to as "bureaucharisma" in organizational settings.

The impulse- and process-oriented postmodern self can be interpreted as a part of a twentieth-century charismatic movement that bears the distinctive stamp of modern culture: individualism and the truth of the senses. The same process of rationalization and disenchantment that led to the decline and secularization of the the spirit of Christian asceticism laid the groundwork for a new search for the fundamental, the essential, and the center of human existence. The postmodern charismatic is based above all on individual experience: experience of self, experience of emotion, and experience of the senses. The modern world bears irrevocably the stamp of an enterprise completely revolutionary and tradition-breaking, yet which holds at the same time absolute faith in the canon that truth must be established on the basis of the individual's experience. The weltanschauung of science and the spirit of the postmodern self may be worlds apart on all issues save one. But they agree wholeheartedly on at least one truth: individual experience is the touchstone against which all else is to be judged.

ALTERNATIVE FORMS OF THE POSTMODERN SELF: THERAPEUTIC ETHIC AND ORGANIZATIONAL PROCESS

As the final component of our recasting of postmodern self theory we turn to consideration of the specific nature of the postmodern self. We offer a reformulation which can incorporate aspects of theory and research on contemporary self-concept not taken into consideration by previous postmodern self arguments.

The theoretical formulation used to direct the research of personal documents organized the various postmodern statements into two dimensions and portrayed postmodern self arguments as describing a shift from Institution to Impulse, and from Product to Process. The two dimensions were argued to be independent yet related axes. In reformulating the theory we will focus on relationships among the analytical dimensions not explicitly addressed by postmodern self arguments or by our previous consideration of the theory. Figure 11.1 shows the postmodern self meaning dimensions, and will be referred to in the discussion.

Agreement among the different variants of the postmodern self predictions was expressed in a general theoretical formulation which was used to structure the research effort. The research was concerned with what would be termed, in Figure 11.1, the *consistent* cells, that is, with a shift from an Institution-Product self (cell a) to an Impulse-Process self (cell d).

We observed that the results of the study of personal documents indicated not so much the emergence of a well-defined postmodern type as the decay of an older self-system. The nuances and ambiguities of the qualitative and quantitative analyses suggest a more complex state of affairs than a simple two-state shift from modern to postmodern. Is it possible that there are alternate forms of the postmodern self, an

Figure 11.1
Analytical Dimensions of the Postmodern Self

	INSTITUTION	IMPULSE
PRODUCT	(a)	(b)
PROCESS	(c)	(d)

```
The Postmodern Self Argument Describes a Shift from
Cell (a) to Cell (d).


Alternative Forms of the Postmodern Self:
Therapeutic Ethic - Cell (b) and Organizational Process - Cell (c)
```

Impulse-Product type (cell b), or an Institution-Process self (cell c)? Can evidence for the empirical occurrence of these alternative forms be found?

Although they are not explicitly recognized in postmodern self arguments, each of the inconsistent types represents a phenomenon which has been considered in other works on contemporary self and character, and which is furthermore in evidence in the contemporary United States. We suggest that these types be considered alternative forms of the postmodern self, and term them, respectively, *therapeutic ethic* and *organizational process*.

Rieff (1966) described the emergence of a "therapeutic ethic" in Western society (see also Schneider and Zurcher, 1970). The triumph of the therapeutic was the eclipsing of earlier modes of character by the "doctrines of psychological man"—goal-oriented, calculated pursuit of impulse release (Rieff, 1966:10–17). In the present terminology the therapeutic orientation as expressed in a self-concept would be an Impulse-Product self, cell b in Figure 11.1. The therapeutic ethic was de-

scribed more recently as an empirically occurring self-concept or character type by Bellah et al. (1985), who observed that it had penetrated
deeply into middle-class mainstream culture (p. 102). The therapeutic
attitude begins with the self rather than with a set of external obligations;
a goal-oriented, rational attitude is taken toward impulse release. The
therapeutic attitude liberates individuals from the artificial constraints
of social roles, parents, and social institutions by redefining the authentic
self as consisting of the experience and expression of feelings (Bellah,
et al., 1985:98–102).

The inherent contradiction in the therapeutic ethic revolves around
the importation of the formal, rational contractual structure of the economic and bureaucratic world into intimate and personal relations (Bellah et al., 1985: 127). Moral questions and the rigorous discipline of
moral life are transformed by the therapeutic ethic into means-ends,
cost-benefit analysis where individuals are beholden and responsible
only to themselves. But the therapeutic ethic does not promote individual laxity. On the contrary, a new and demanding discipline is imposed
in place of the trials of a moral life and the difficulties of moral choices.
Extreme demands for rational calculation are made on individuals for
insight into values and plans of action of other persons, for self-ac-
counting, and for calculation about outcomes (Bellah et al., 1985:129–
130). Bellah et al. observed that the precepts of the therapeutic attitude
sound not altogether different from a textbook description of decision
making in a school of management. By defining how a "healthy" person
lives, the therapeutic ethic defines by implication how everyone ought
to live, which helps explain the force and extent of this orientation in
contemporary society.

The remaining "inconsistent" combination of the postmodern self analytical dimensions is cell c in Figure 11.1, or Institution-Process. Given
the theoretical dimensions which define this type it can be described in
terms of an attachment and valuation of social roles and institutions,
but where the individual's relationship to such roles and structures is
seen as existing in series, a process of succession where the individual's
orientation toward any given role or organization is never permanent.

There is some indication that just this orientation has emerged among
the younger cohorts of individuals staffing contemporary corporate organizations (Leinberger, 1986). The orientation and values of this new
organization person can best be defined in contrast with the historical
predecessor.

The "organization man" of the 1950s described by William H. Whyte
(1957) made a permanent, frequently lifelong contract with the corpo-
ration, exchanging talent and toil for financial security and a sense of
belonging. The organization man "left home, spiritually as well as phys-

ically, to take the vows of organizational life"; he not only worked for the organization, he belonged to it (Whyte, 1957:3).

The new generation "organization man" is different. According to Leinberger (1986), who conducted follow-up research with Whyte's original subjects and their families, the changed economic and corporate climate of the 1980s has weakened the loyalty ties that contemporary organizational professionals feel toward their companies. More to the point, a changed orientation toward the organization is especially marked among the generation born after World War II. For these individuals and many like them the permanent contract entered into by corporate personnel of the previous generation no longer exists. The following illustrative quotations are from the thirty-three- and thirty-six-year-old sons of one of the respondents in Whyte's original study (Leinberger, 1986:98): (1) "I don't have any loyalty to the company. I'm in it for me. I expect a payout in one fashion or another, in money or in a work environment I have more control over. I see a company as a vehicle"; (2) "Corporate loyalty does not come into the equation. Unless I continue to be excited about what I am doing, I would see no reason to stay."

Whyte (1986:98), in a rejoinder and comment on Leinberger's research, stressed that contemporary corporate professionals resemble their 1950s counterparts in that they do have faith in and loyalty to the larger system: "indeed, today's M.B.A.'s and young urban professionals exhibit a faith in the system every bit as staunch as that of the junior executives of former years." What is different, according to Whyte, is that contemporary corporate professionals have what we have termed a Process orientation toward themselves in relation to the organization rather than a Product orientation. The difference between the old "organization man" and the new is not organizational loyalty per se, but loyalty to a particular organization. This critical difference is spelled out by Whyte:

It is true that he may be less inclined to give his loyalty to one organization. His allegiance now is to organizations. When he speaks of being free to go where his self-interest leads, he is citing the interchangeability of organization life. To use a vogue term, if he "networks," it is not just within one organization, but across a complex of them (Whyte, 1986:98).

The contemporary corporate professional is firmly ensconced in an institutional structure, but at the same time holds no permanent allegiance to any particular company or job.

CONCLUSION: CHALLENGES FOR FURTHER THEORIZING AND RESEARCH

The purpose of this book has been two-fold: to advance theoretical and substantive knowledge about self and social change and to advance procedures for comparative analysis of personal documents. The second purpose has been intended to inform the first.

We have proposed a typology for identifying and classifying key analytical dimensions of self concept and social change (Institution-Impulse/Product-Process). We have arranged the typology in a four-fold table, thereby enabling a description of shifts between and among self-orientations over time. This process has been useful at least demonstratively. But there is a need for further comparative cases to validate the typology cells and to fill them more fully. Are there other cells beyond the four which we identified? What information about the balance of product/process and institution/impulse can be gained by studies of the self-concept of individuals in varying occupations and professions, in varying stages of the life cycle, and as reflected in other demographic differences like sex, ethnicity, and socioeconomic status?

Is there an ideal balance of self-concept, among Product-Process and Institution-Impulse under any given conditions or rate of social change? If the postmodern self does characterize a charismatic movement in modern culture, what other evidence is there of that phenomenon at the individual, group, community, organizational, and societal levels? What is the nature of the modern self which is presupposed or assumed by postmodern self theories? How is the postmodern self, or any configuration of Product-Process and Institution-Impulse internalized by the individual from experienced elements of social change? What is the complete nature of the dialectical aspects of product versus process and institution versus impulse cognitively for individuals and socially among individuals? How do Institution-Impulse and Product-Process relate to analytical schemes like other-directed (Riesman, 1961), narcissistic self (Lasch, 1979), and similar theoretical configurations of self-concept?

Since much of our book has concentrated on reactions to social change in terms of self-concept, a reasonable question for further theory and research concerns the efficacious balance of Institution-Impulse and Product-Process in the self-concepts of individuals who are proactive in their social environments. Such individuals would be change agents rather than reactors to change. What is the pragmatic self-concept for change agents and for what kinds of changes in what sort of milieu? How do individuals move back and forth between proaction and reaction vis-à-vis social change? Do they define their true or real selves differently when proacting as compared with reacting? We have mentioned several times that because of sample limitations we have attempted to affect analytical generalization from our findings; that is generalizing to theory. Several of these extrapolations are presented earlier in this chapter and in Chapter 10. The questions we have just outlined are intended to stimulate studies which will provide data enabling sample to population generalizations.

The computer-assisted analysis of personal documents, in our case diaries, seems to have been an effective technique for revealing reported changes in self-concept over time. Again with caution about the limitations of the study sample, we argue that the dictionary and the content analysis protocol, with the computer program, developed for our research are good examples of how the task of gleaning information about self-concept and social change from personal documents can be conducted. More elaborate dictionaries need to be developed, more comprehensive samples of text need to be employed, and more elaborate comparisons need to be undertaken. In addition to diaries, such personal documents as letters, memos, autobiographies, memoirs, audio or visual recordings, fiction, song, poetry, and other manifestations of the interaction betweeen biography and society can be useful sources of information about self-concept and social change. We hope this book will have encouraged and facilitated such endeavors.

NOTES

1. Chapter 2 contains a discussion of formal and substantive rationality, which we will not repeat here.

2. We have discussed the concept of ideal type under the heading of "typological representativeness" in Chapter 6.

Appendix A

Content Analysis Dictionary

INSTITUTION CATEGORIES

FAMILY

aunt aunt's aunts brother brother's brothers child children children's child's childs dad daddies daddy dad's dads daughter daughter's daughters divorce divorced divorces divorcing engaged engagement families family family's father father's fathers folk folks grandchild grandchildren grandchildren's grandchild's grandfather grandfather's grandmother grandmother's home homes household households husband husband's husbands in-law kid kid's kids marital marriage marriages married marry marrying marrys mother mother's mothers parent parent's parents related relation relative relative's relatives sister sister's sisters son son's sons uncle uncle's uncles wedding weddings widow widow's widows wife wife's wives

COMMUN

band bands block blocks center centers circle circles cities citizen citizens city club clubs communities community cooperative cooperatives district districts join joined joining neighbor neighborhood neighbors town towns village villages

NATNL

america american americans brother brothers citizen citizens civil country culture cultures folk international kingdom kingdom's nation nation's nations national nationals nations north northern north's people people's peoples population populations public race races region regional regions south south's southern state states territories territory united

HUMAN

cultural culture cultures folk generation generations humanity international mankind masses social societies society world worlds

WORK

build building builds built busier busiest busily busy career careers construct constructed construction earn earned earning earns employed employee employees employer employers employment farm farmed farmer farmers farming farms fire fired fires firing industries industry job jobs labor labors local locals mine mined mines mining occupation occupational pay payed paying pays plant planted planting plants produce produced producer producers produces producing product production productive productivity products profession professional professions service serviced services servicing shift shifts skill skilled skills strike strikes striking struck till tills trade trades union unions work worked worker worker's workers working works

RELIG

angel angels baptist belief beliefs believe believed believes believing bible biblical bless blessed blessing brother brothers catholic catholicism christ christ's christian christianity church churches devotion divine divinity faith faithful god god's grace heaven heavenly heavens holy jew judaism light lights lord lord's meeting meetings methodist minister ministers ministry offering pious pray prayed prayer prayers preach preacher preaches priest priests protestant protestantism religion religions religious revere revered reverence reverend reverent reveres sacred saint salvation sermon sermons service services soul souls spirit spiritual teaching teachings temple testament trial trials worship worshipped worshipping worships

POLIT

bill bills campaign campaigning campaigns candidate candidates capitol congress congresses conservative conservatives convention conventions democracies democracy democrat democratic democrats elect elected electing election elections elects federal government governmental governments house king kingdom kingdoms kings labor left legislation legislative legislature liberal liberals minister ministers parties party platform platforms policies policy political politically politician politicians politics president president's presidents primaries primary race races representative representatives republic republican republicans republics right secretaries secretary service state states tax taxed taxes taxing taxpayer taxpayers union

ECO/BUS

account accounting accounts afford afforded affording affords bank banked bankers banking banks benefit benefits bill bills bought business businesses businessman businessmen buy buyer buyers buying buys capital capitalism charge charged charges charging check checks companies company concern concerns cost costly costs credit credits deal dealer dealers dealing deals dollar dollars due dues earnings economic economics economy exchange exchanges expense expenses finance financed financial financially financing firm firms fund funds gain gains goods interest loan loans market marketing markets merchant merchants monetary money moneys office offices own owned owner owners owning owns pay payed paying payment payments pays pound pounds profit profitable profitably property purchase purchased purchases purchasing saving savings secretaries secretary securities security shop shopped shopping shops sold spend spending spends spent store stored stores storing trade traded trades trading worth

FORM/ORG

agencies agency association associations commission commissions committee committees conference conferences congress convention conventions department departments facilities facility institute institutes institution institutions member members memberships movement movements organization organizations society

EDUC

academic campus class classes classroom college colleges educate educated educates educating education educational faculty grade graded grades grading graduate graduated graduates graduating graduation instructor instructors professor professors scholar scholars scholarships school schooling schools secondary student students studies study studying taught teach teacher teachers teaches teaching teachings train trained training trains universities university

SOC/CLASS

class classes club clubs country culture cultured discrimination educated force forced forces forcing fortune fortunes high higher influence influenced influences influencing low lower middle peasant peasants poor poorer poorest poverty power powerful powers pressure pressured pressures pressuring prestige prominent push pushed pushes pushing rank ranks rich richer riches richest segregation society status statuses success successful wealth wealthy welfare

AMB/ACH

abilities ability able accomplish accomplished accomplishes accomplishing ac-

complishment accomplishments achieve achieved achievement achievements
achieves achieving aim aimed aiming aims ambition ambitions ambitious attain
attained attaining attainment attainments attains attempt attempted attempting
attempts capabilities capability capable capacities capacity devote devoted devotes devoting drive drives driving drove effect effected effecting effects end
ended ending ends goal goals object objective objectives objects progress progressed progressing project projects purpose purposes pursue pursued pursues
pursuing resolution resolve resolved resolves resolving task tasks

RTNAL

advice advise advised argument arrange arranged arrangement arrangements
arranges arranging choice choices choose choosing chosen conduct conducted
conducting conducts conscious consciously consider considerations considered
considering considers decide decided decides deciding decision decisions explain
explained explaining explains explanation explanations figure figured figures
figuring handle handled handles handling intellectual intellectuals intelligence
intelligent intend intended intending intends intent intention intentions judgement judgements manage managed manages managing master mastered mas-
tering masters pattern patterned patterns plan planned planning plans program
programs project projected projecting projection projections projects proposal
proposals propose proposed proposes proposing rational rationale reason reasonable reasonably reasoned reasoning reasons recognize recognizes smart
smarter smartest solution solutions suppose supposed supposes supposing
think thinking thinks will willing willingly wills wisdom wise wiser wisest

LEAD

administration administrative administrator authorities authority authorized
board boards boss bosses chair chaired chairman chancellor charge chief chiefs
command commanded commander commanders commanding commands dominant dominate dominated dominates dominating dominatingly domination
head heads lead leader leaders leadership leading leads manager managers
master masters office officer officers offices official officials order ordered or-
dering orders president president's presidents rule rules ruler rules ruling under

LAW/RUL

act acts arrest arrested arresting arrests attorney attorneys bar court courts jail
jailed jailing jails judge judged judges judging judicial law laws lawyer lawyers
legal legislation officer officers official principle principles prison prisoner pris-
oners prisons qualification qualifications qualified qualify regulation regulations
rule ruled rules ruling standard standards trial trials

RSPN/DUT

accord accordance according accordingly adjust adjusted adjusting adjustment adjustments commit commiting commitment commits committed compulsive conform conformity conforms contract contracts debt debts due duties duty follow followed following follows indebted liability liable must obey obeyed obeying obeys obligated obligation obligations oblige obliged observe observed observes observing ought responsibilities responsibility responsible

IMPULSE CATEGORIES

SENSE

ate color coloring colors contact contacts drink drinking drinks ear ears eat eaten eating eats eye eyes feast feasted feasting feasts feel feeling feels felt hear heard hearing hears image images listen listened listening listens look looked looking looks mouth mouths observation observe observed observes observing see seeing seen sees sensation sensations sense sensed senses sensing sensitive sensitivity sight sights silence silent silently smell smelled smelling smells stomach taste tasted tastes tasting touch touched touches touching watch watched watches watching

E/AROUS

affect affected affecting affects anxious anxiously appeal appealed appealing appeals desire desired desires desiring emotion emotional emotionally emotions enthusiasm enthusiastic excite excited excitement excites exciting fascinate fascinated fascinates fascinating fascination feel feeling feelings feels felt inspire inspired inspires inspiring interest interested interesting interests mood moods moody move moved moves moving nervous nervously nervousness passion passionate passions refreshing spirit spirits stimulate stimulated stimulates stimulating stimulation stimulus stirring thrill thrilled thrilling urge urged urges urging

E/AFFCT

admirable admirably admiration admire admired admires admiring affection affectionate affectionately affections buddies buddy cherish cherished close closer closest court courted courting courts darling dear dearer dearest devote devoted devotes devotion embrace embraced embraces embracing fellowship fellowships fond fonder fondly fondness friend friendly friends friendship friendships honey honeymoon intimate intimately kiss kissed kisses kissing like liked likes liking love loved lover lovers loves loving regard regards romance romances romantic sweet sweeter sweetest sweetheart sweethearts sweetly trust trusted trusting trusts warm warmed warmer warmest warming warmly warms warmth

E/PLEAS

agreeable amuse amused amusement amuses amusing attractive beautiful beautifully beauty charm charming cheerful cheerfully comfort comfortable comfortably congenial content contented delight delighted delightful enjoy enjoyed enjoying enjoyment enjoys entertain entertained entertaining entertainment fair fairer fairest favorable favorite fun funnier funniest funny gay glad happier happiest happily happiness happy humor humour joy joys lovely nice nicely nicer nicest pleasant pleasantly please pleased pleases pleasing pleasure pleasures prettier prettiest prettily pretty satisfaction satisfactions satisfied satisfies satisfy satisfying welcome welcomed welcomes welcoming

E/DSTRSS

afraid alarm alarmed alienate alienated alienation anxieties anxiety anxious anxiously apprehension blue blues concern concerned concerning concerns cried cries cry crying depress depressed depressing depression depressions despair disturb disturbed disturbing disturbs dread dreaded dreadful fear feared fearing fears frighten frightened frightening frightens gloom gloomingly grief guilt guilty horror melancholy nerves nervous nervously nervousness panic regret regrets regretted regretting sad scare scared scares scaring sorrow sorrows sorry suffer suffered suffering suffers tension tensions terror trouble troubled troubles troubling weep weeping weeps wept worried worries worry worrying

E/ANGR

anger angered angering angers angrier angriest angry annoy annoyance annoyed annoying contempt contemptible cross disgust disgusted disgusting disgustingly dislike disliked dislikes disliking furious furiously fury hate hated hates hating hatred hostile indignant indignation mad madden rage raged rages resent resented resentful resentment temper

MOTV

appetite appetites drive drives driving drove hungry impulse impulses instinct instinctive instinctively instincts motivate motivated motivation motive motives need needed needing needs sex sexes sexual

IRRAT

absurd absurdities absurdity alien crazier craziest craziness crazy dream dreamer dreaming dreams dreamt fantasies fantasy hysteria hysterical illusion illusions insane insanity intuition intuitions intuitive irrational irrationality mad mania maniac meaningless mystic mystical mysticism mystics neurotic nonsense silly

EXPER

appear appearance appearances appeared appearing appears aware awareness conscious consciously consciousness experience experienced experiences experiencing note noted notes notice notices noticing noting observe observed observer observers observes observing perceive perceived perceives sense sensed senses sensing sensitive sensitivity sensory subject subjected subjecting subjective subjects survey surveyed surveying surveys undergo undergoes undergoing undergone underwent

DEV

against argue argued argues arguing argument arguments block blocked blocking blocks conflict conflicting conflicts contrary contrast contrasts counter denied denies deny denying deviant deviants deviation deviations difference differences different differently discrepancies discrepancy divergent diverse diversity exception exceptional exceptions irregular irregularities irregularly mix mixed mixes mixing object objected objecting objects opponent opponents oppose opposed opposes opposing opposite opposition paradox paradoxical paradoxically puzzling strange strangely unusual unusually wander wandered wandering wanders

NATRL

display displayed displaying displays escape escaped escapes escaping frank free freed freedoms freeing freely frees independence liberty loose loosely natural naturally open opened openly opens release released releases releasing

NOV/SPON

casual casually chance chanced ease easier easiest easily easy fresh informal informally new newer newest newly novel novelties readily readiness relax relaxation relaxed spontaneity spontaneous spontaneously surprise surprised surprises surprising surprisingly unexpected unexpectedly unprecedented

PRODUCT CATEGORIES

STRUCT

base based bases basic basically basing basis build builds built construct constructed construction figure figures form formation formed forming forms foundation foundations frame framed frames framework framing mold molded molding molds object objects order organization organize organized organizes organizing settle shape shaped shapes shaping structural structure structured structures structuring system systematic systematically systems

EVER

consistent consistently constant constantly continual continue continued continues continuing continuity continuous continuously convention conventional conventions custom customary customs daily duration endless endlessly established ever everyday fixed habit habits keep keeping keeps kept last lasted lasting lasts maintain maintained maintaining maintains norm norms permanent permanently persist persisted persistence persistent practice practices prolong prolonged prolonging prolongs regular regularly routine settled stability stable stay stayed staying stays steadily steady usual usually

GOOD

character characters conscience conscientious correct corrected correcting corrects courage decency decent ethic ethical ethics fair fairly generous generously gentleman gentlemen goodness handsome honest honestly honesty honor honorable honored honoring honors innocence innocent integrity judge judged judges judging just justice kind kindly ladies lady moral morality morals noble nobler nobles perfect perfection perfectly polite politely politeness proper properly propriety pure purity qualities quality reputable reputation respect respectable respected respecting respects right sincere sincerity standard standards virtue virtues

BAD

ashamed awful bad badly badness bastard bastards corrupt corruption crude cruel cruelty curse cursed damn damned devil devils dirty evil evils gross hell hideous horrible ill mean shame sin sins terrible ugliness ugly unfair vice vices vulgar wicked wickedly wickedness worse worst wrong

COMPLETE

cap caps close closed closes closing complete completed completely completes completing completion conclude concluded concludes concluding conclusion conclusions consequence consequences consequent end ended ending endings ends final finally finish finished finishes finishing last limit limits outcome outcomes output outputs product production products succeed succeeding succeeds terminal terminate termination

INCOMP

arrest arrested arresting arrests cancel cancelled cancelling cancels fraction fractions halt halted incomplete incompletely interrupt interrupted interrupting interruption partial partially postpone postponed stop stopped stopping stops suspend suspended

PROCESS CATEGORIES

BLUR

blur blurred chaos chaotic confuse confused confuses confusing confusion doubt doubted doubtful doubting doubts indefinite indefinitely mysteries mysterious mystery obscure obscured obscurity puzzle puzzled random uncertain uncertainty unknown

VARY

alteration alterations altered alternate bend bending bends bent change changed changes changing cycle cycles flexibility flexible periodic periodically shift shifted shifting shifts transience transition transitional transitions unstructured variable variation variations varied varies varieties variety various vary varying

MANY

aggregate blend blended blends bunch bundle bundles cluster clustered clustering clusters compound compounds hundred hundreds lot lots manifold many mass masses million miscellaneous mixed mixture multiple multiplicity multiplied multiplies multiply multiplying myriad numerous

PRCSS

advance advanced advances advancing became become becomes becoming flow flowed flowing flows grow growing grown grows growth move moved movement movements moves moving proceed proceeded proceeding proceeds process processed processes processing sequence sequences series succession successive

EVNT

act acted acting action actions active actively activities activity acts behave behaved behaves behaving behavior event events exist existed existence existing exists function functioned functioning functions happen happened happening happens incident incidents instance instances manner mode modes motion motions perform performance performances performed performing performs react reacted reacting reaction reactions reacts respond responded responding responds response responses treat treated treating treatment treatments treats

DISC

clarified clarify clarity clue clues detect detected detecting detects disclose disclosed discloses discover discovered discoveries discovering discovers discovery evident evidently examine examined examines examining exploration explore explored explores exploring expose exposed exposes exposing exposure exposures find finding finds found locate located quest reveal revealed revealing reveals search searched searches searching secret secrets seek seeking seeks sought

UNCLASSIFIED CATEGORIES

T/PST

age aged ages aging ago ancient before earlier earliest early elder elderly elders eldest former formerly historian historians historical history late memorable memorial memories memory old older oldest past previous previously prior recall recalled recalling recalls senior tradition traditional traditionally yesterday

T/FUT

forthcoming future futures tomorrow

T/PRES

now present presently time today today's

INDIV

being beings identities identity individual individualism individuality individually individuals person personal personalities personality personally persons temper temperament

RESTRAIN

compose composed composes composure confine confined confines confining constrain constrained constraining constrains constraint control controlled controlling controls curb curbing curbs discrete discretely inhibit inhibited inhibiting inhibition inhibitions inhibits reserved restrain restrained restraining restrains restraint restraints restrict restricted restricting restriction restrictions restricts subdue subdued suppress suppressed suppression temperate

Appendix B

Diary Bibliographic Sources
Not Cited in Text

Besterman, 1965–1966
Bowker, 1967
Chicorel, 1974
Forbes, 1967
Gale, 1965
Gohdes, 1970
International Sociological Association, 1955
Leary, 1954
MacPike, E. F., 1944–1945
Nicholsen, 1969
Nilon, 1970
Publishers Trade List Annual, 1957
Sheehy, 1976
Spiller, 1974
Wilson, 1937–1942

Bibliography

Adams, Charles Francis
    1964a   Diary of Charles Francis Adams. Volume 1. January 1820-June 1825. Edited by Aida DiPace Donald and David Donald. Cambridge: The Belknap Press of Harvard University Press.
    1964b   Diary of Charles Francis Adams. Volume 2. July 1825-September 1829. Edited by Aida DiPace Donald and David Donald. Cambridge: The Belknap Press of Harvard University Press.

Adamski, Wladyslaw W.
    n.d.   "Memoir Sociology: Between Intutitive and Quantitative Orientations." Unpublished manuscript, Institute of Philosophy and Sociology of the Polish Academy of Sciences.

Adler, Nathan
    1968   "The antinomian personality: The hippie character type." Psychiatry 31:325–338.
    1972   The Underground Stream: New Life Styles and the Antinomian Personality. New York: Harper and Row/Harper Torchbooks.

Allport, Gordon W.
    1942   The Use of Personal Documents in Psychological Science. New York: Social Science Research Council.

American Bibliographical Center
    1964   America: History and Life. Volume 1. Santa Barbara: American Bibliographical Center-Clio Press.

Angell, Robert C., and Ronald Freeman
    1953   "The use of documents, records, census materials, and indices." In Research Methods in the Behavioral Sciences, L. Festinger and D. Katz, pp. 300–326. New York: Dryden Press.

Anonymous
    1971   Go Ask Alice. New York: Prentice-Hall/Avon.
Ashton, T.S.
    1976   The Industrial Revolution 1760–1830. London: Oxford University
            Press.
Baldwin, Christopher Columbus
    1901   Diary of Christopher Columbus Baldwin, Librarian of the American
            Antiquarian Society 1829–1835. Volume 8. Transactions and Collec-
            tions of the American Antiquarian Society.
Barbour, Martha Isabella Hopkins
    1936   Journals of the Late Brevet Major Philip Norbourne Barbour, and his
            wife, Martha Isabella Hopkins Barbour. Written during the war with
            Mexico–1846. Edited with foreword by Rhoda Van Bibber Tanner
            Doubleday. New York: G. P. Putnam's Sons.
Barton, Michael Lee
    1974   "The Character of Civil War Soldiers: A Comparative Analysis of the
            Language of Moral Evaluation in Diaries." Ph.D. dissertation, Uni-
            versity of Pennsylvania.
Bell, Daniel
    1976   The Coming of the Post-Industrial Society: A Venture in Social Fore-
            casting. Foreword to paperback edition, copyright 1976. New York:
            Basic Books/Harper Colophon.
    1978   The Cultural Contradictions of Capitalism. Foreword to paperback
            edition, copyright 1978. New York: Basic Books/Harper Colophon.
Bellah, Robert N., Richard Madsen, William M. Sullivan, Ann Swidler, and
            Steven M. Tipton
    1985   Habits of the Heart: Individualism and Commitment in American
            Life. New York: Harper & Row.
Benedict, Ruth
    1959   An Anthropologist at Work: Writings of Ruth Benedict. Edited by
            Margaret Mead. New York: Equinox/Avon.
Bennett, Joan Frances
    1970   Members of the Class Will Keep Daily Journals: The Barnard College
            Journals of Tobi Gillian Sanders and Joan Frances Bennett, Spring
            1968. New York: Winter House.
Berelson, Bernard R.
    1954   "Content analysis." In Handbook of Social Psychology, edited by G.
            Lindzey, vol. 1, pp. 488–518. Reading, Mass.: Addison-Wesley.
Berger, Josef, and Dorothy Berger (eds.)
    1957   Diary of America. New York: Simon and Schuster.
Berger, Peter L., Brigitte Berger, and Hansfried Kellner
    1973   The Homeless Mind: Modernization and Consciousness. New York:
            Random House/Vintage.
Berkhofer, Robert F., Jr.
    1969   A Behavioral Approach to Historical Analysis. New York: Free Press.
Bernal, J. D.
    1969   Science and Industry in the Nineteenth Century. Bloomington: In-
            diana University Press.

Bertaux, Daniel (ed.)
  1981   Biography and Society: The Life History Approach. The Social Sciences Sage Studies in International Sociology, no. 23. Beverly Hills: Sage.
Besterman, Theodore
  1965–66 A World Bibliography of Bibliographies and of Bibliographical Catalogues, Calendars, Abstracts, Digests, Indexes, and the Like. Fourth edition, revised, and greatly enlarged throughout. Lausanne: Societas Bibliographica.
Birnbaum, Norman
  1971   Toward a Critical Sociology. London: Oxford University Press.
Blumer, Herbert
  1939   "An appraisal of Thomas and Znaniecki's *The Polish Peasant in Europe and America*." Critiques of Research in the Social Sciences I. New York: Social Science Research Council.
Bogdan, Robert, and Steven J. Taylor
  1975   Introduction to Qualitative Research Methods: A Phenomenological Approach to the Social Sciences. New York: Wiley-Interscience.
Bouchard, Thomas J., Jr.
  1976   "Unobtrusive measures: An inventory of uses." Sociological Methods and Research 4:267–300.
Boulding, Kenneth E.
  1964   The Meaning of the Twentieth Century: The Great Transition. New York: Harper and Row.
Bowker, R.R.
  1967   The Library Journal Book Review. New York: R.R. Bowker.
  1977   The Reader's Adviser. 12th ed. New York: R.R. Bowker.
Braverman, Harry
  1974   Labor and Monopoly Capital: The Degradation of Work in the Twentieth Century. New York: Monthly Review Press.
Bremer, Arthur H.
  1972   An Assassin's Diary. Introduction by Harding Lemay. New York: Harper's Magazine Press.
Brent, Edward
  1984   "Qualitative computing: Approaches and issues." Qualitative Sociology 7:34–60.
Brown, William R.
  1939   Minnesota Farmers' Diaries: William R. Brown, 1845–1846; Mitchell Young Jackson, 1852–1853. Introduction and notes by Rodney C. Loehr. St. Paul: Minnesota Historical Society.
Browning, Harley L., and Joachim Singelmann
  1975   "The Emergence of a Service Society: Demographic and Sociological Aspects of the Sectoral Transformation of the Labor Force in the U.S.A." Springfield, Va.: National Technical Information Service.
Browning, Orville Hickman
  1925   The Diary of Orville Hickman Browning. Volume 1. 1850–1864. Edited with introduction and notes by Theodore Calvin Pease and James G.

            Randall. Collections of the Illinois State Historical Library. Vol. XX.
            Springfield, Ill.: Trustees of the Illinois State Historical Library.
Brubaker, Roger
    1984   The Limits of Rationality: An Essay on the Social and Moral Thought
            of Max Weber. London: Allen and Unwin.
Brzezinski, Zbigniew
    1970   Between Two Ages: America's Role in the Technetronic Era. New
            York: Viking.
Bukowski, Jacek
    1974   "Biographical method in Polish sociology." Zeitschrift fur Soziologie
            3:18–30.
Butterfield, Stephen
    1974   Black Autobiography in America. Amherst: University of Massachu-
            setts Press.
Campbell, Joseph (ed.)
    1971   The Portable Jung. Edited with introduction by J. Campbell. Trans-
            lated by R. F. C. Hull. New York: Viking.
Cavan, Ruth Shonle
    1929   "Topical summaries of current literature: Interviewing for life-history
            material." American Journal of Sociology 35:100–115.
Cawelti, John G.
    1974   "Myth, symbol, and formula." Journal of Popular Culture 8:1–9.
Chalasinski, Jozef
    1981   "The life records of the young generation of polish peasants as a
            manifestation of contemporary culture." In Biography and Society,
            edited by Daniel Bertaux, pp. 119–132. Sage Studies in International
            Sociology, no. 23. Beverly Hills: Sage.
Chicorel, Marietta
    1974   Chicorel Index to Biographies. 1st ed. New York: Chicorel Library.
Cipolla, Carlo M.
    1974   The Economic History of World Population. 6th ed. Baltimore: Pen-
            guin.
Clark, Laura Downs
    1920   "The original diary of Mrs. Laura (Downs) Clark, of Wakeman Ohio."
            From June 21 to October 26, 1818. The Firelands Pioneer n.s. XXI
            (January):2308–2326.
Clecak, Peter
    1983   America's Quest for the Ideal Self: Dissent and Fulfillment in the 60s
            and 70s. New York: Oxford University Press.
Cleveland, Charles E.
    1985   QUESTER. West DesMoines, Iowa: Communication Development
            Company.
Clough, Shephard B., and Carol G. Moodie (eds.)
    1965   European Economic History: Documents and Readings. Princeton:
            D. Van Nostrand.
Collins, Randall
    1980   "Weber's last theory of capitalism: A systemization." American So-
            ciological Review 45:925–942.

Curtis, William Edmond
 1926 Letters and Journals. Judge William Edmund, 1755–1838; Judge Hol-
brook Curtis, 1787–1858; Judge William Edmond Curtis, 1823–1880;
William Edmond Curtis, 1855–1923; and Dr. Holbrook Curtis, 1856–
1920. Compiled by Elizabeth Curtis. Hartford: Case, Lockwood and
Brainard.
Deane, Phyllis
 1965 The First Industrial Revolution. Cambridge, England: Cambridge
University Press.
Degler, Carl N.
 1977 The Age of the Economic Revolution 1876–1900. 2d ed. Glenview,
Ill.: Scott, Foresman.
Dennis, Deborah L.
 1984 "'Word crunching': An annotated bibliography on computers and
qualitative data analysis." Qualitative Sociology 7:148–156.
Dewey, John
 1916 Democracy and Education: An Introduction to the Philosophy of
Education. New York: Free Press.
 1922 Human Nature and Conduct: An Introduction to Social Psychology.
New York: Modern Library.
Dilthey, Wilhelm
 1961 Pattern and Meaning in History: Thoughts on History and Society.
Edited with introduction by H. P. Rickman. New York: Harper and
Row/Harper Torchbooks.
Dunaway, Philip, and Mel Evans (eds.)
 1957 A Treasury of the World's Great Diaries. Introduction by Louis Un-
termeyer. New York: Doubleday.
Duncan, Elizabeth Caldwell
 1928 Diary of Mrs. Joseph Duncan (Elizabeth Caldwell Smith). Edited with
introduction by Elizabeth Duncan Putnam. Journal of the Illinois State
Historical Society 21:1–91.
Dunphy, Dexter C.
 1966 "Social change in self-analytic groups." In The General Inquirer, P.
J. Stone et al., pp. 287–340. Cambridge: M.I.T.
Eisenstadt, S. N.
 1968 "Introduction." In Max Weber on Charisma and Institution Building:
Selected Papers, pp. ix-lvi. Edited with introduction by S. N. Eisenstadt. Chicago: University of Chicago Press.
 1973 Tradition, Change, and Modernity. New York: Wiley.
Engels, Frederick
 1958 The Condition of the Working Class in England. Translated and ed-
ited by W. O. Henderson and W.H. Chaloner. Stanford: Stanford
University Press.
Erickson, Rosemary J., Waymon J. Crow, Louis A. Zurcher, Jr., and Archie V.
Connett
 1973 Paroled But Not Free. New York: Behavioral Publications.
Erikson, Erik H.
 1963 Childhood and Society. New York: Norton.

Faris, Robert E. L.
  1970   Chicago Sociology 1920–1932. Foreword by Morris Janowitz. Chicago
            and London: University of Chicago Press-Phoenix.
Fisher, Sidney George
  1967   A Philadelphia Perspective: The Diary of Sidney George Fisher Cov-
            ering the Years 1834–1871. Edited by Nicholas B. Wainwright. Phil-
            adelphia: Historical Society of Pennsylvania.
Fletcher, Calvin
  1972   The Diary of Calvin Fletcher. Volume 1. 1817–1838. Including letters
            of Calvin Fletcher and diaries and letters of his wife Sarah Hill
            Fletcher. Edited by Gayle Thornbrough. Indianapolis: Indiana His-
            torical Society.
Forbes, Harriette (comp.)
  1967   New England Diaries 1602–1800: A Descriptive Catalog of Diaries,
            Orderly Books and Sea Journals. New York: Russell and Russell.
Fothergill, Robert A.
  1974   Private Chronicles: A Study of English Diaries. London: Oxford Uni-
            versity Press.
Frankfurter, Felix
  1975   From the Diaries of Felix Frankfurter. Biographical essay and notes
            by Joseph P. Lash. Assisted by Jonathan Lash. New York: Norton.
Freidel, Frank (ed.)
  1974   Harvard Guide to American History. Volume 1. Rev. ed. Cambridge:
            The Belknap Press of Harvard University Press.
Freud, Sigmund
  1955   "Analysis of a phobia in a five-year-old boy." In The Standard Edition
            of the Complete Psychological Works of Sigmund Freud, vol. 10, pp.
            3–149. Translated under the general editorship of James Strachey in
            collaboration with Anna Freud. Assisted by Alix Strachey and Alan
            Tyson. London: The Hogarth Press and the Institute of Psychoanal-
            ysis.
  1958   "Psycho-analytic notes on an autobiographical account of a case of
            paranoia (dementia paranoides)." In The Standard Edition, vol. 12,
            pp. 3–85. London: The Hogarth Press and the Institute of Psychoa-
            nalysis.
  1965   New Introductory Lectures on Psychoanalysis. Translated and edited
            by James Strachey. New York: Norton.
Fromm, Erich
  1972   "What does it mean to be human." In Humanistic Society: Today's
            Challenge to Sociology. Edited by John F. Glass and John R. Staude,
            pp. 32–54. Pacific Palisades, Calif.: Goodyear.
Fuchs, Victor R.
  1968   The Service Economy. New York: National Bureau of Economic Re-
            search.
Gag, Wanda
  1940   Growing Pains: Diaries and Drawings for the Years 1908–1917. New
            York: Coward-McCann.

Galbraith, John Kenneth
  1971   The New Industrial State. 2d ed., rev. New York: New American Library/Mentor.
Gale Research Co.
  1965   Book Review Index. Volume 1. Detroit: Gale Research Co.
Gendron, Bernard
  1977   Technology and the Human Condition. New York: St. Martin's Press.
Giddens, Anthony
  1973   The Class Structure of the Advanced Societies. New York: Harper and Row/Harper Torchbooks.
Gohdes, Clarence
  1970   Bibliographical Guide to the Study of the Literature of the U.S.A. 3d ed. Durham: Duke University Press.
Gottschalk, Louis, Clyde Kluckhohn, and Robert Angell
  1945   The Use of Personal Documents in History, Anthropology and Sociology. New York: Social Science Research Council.
Hadley, James
  1951   Diary 1843–1852 of James Hadley, Tutor and Professor of Greek in Yale College, 1845–1872. Edited with foreword by Laura Hadley Mosely. New Haven: Yale University Press.
Hartsough, Ross, and Julius Laffal
  1970   "Content analysis of scientific writings." Journal of General Psychology 83:193–206.
Hartwell, R. M. (ed.)
  1967   The Causes of the Industrial Revolution in England. Edited with introduction by R. M. Hartwell. London: Methuen; New York: Harper and Row/Barnes and Noble.
Hayes, Rutherford Birchard
  1922   Diary and Letters of Rutherford Birchard Hayes, Nineteenth President of the United States. Volume 1. 1834–1860. Edited by Charles Richard Williams. Columbus: Ohio State Archaeological and Historical Society.
Heaton, H.
  1967   "Industrial Revolution." In The Causes of the Industrial Revolution in England, edited by R. M. Hartwell, pp. 31–52. London: Methuen; New York: Harper and Row/Barnes and Noble.
Hewitt, Helen-Jo Jakusz
  1976   Basic Text-Processing Programs: A Manual. With the assistance of Robert A. Amsler. Austin: Humanities Research Center, University of Texas at Austin.
Hinkle, Gisela J.
  1951   "The Role of Freudianism in American Sociology." Ph.D. dissertation, University of Wisconsin.
Hobsbawm, E. J.
  1962   The Age of Revolution 1789–1848. New York: New American Library/Mentor.
  1969   Industry and Empire. Vol. 3, The Pelican Economic History of Britain, "From 1750 to the Present Day." Baltimore: Penguin.

Hochschild, Arlie Russell
  1983   The Managed Heart: Commercialization of Human Feeling. Berkeley:
            University of California Press.
Hollingshead, August B., and Frederick C. Redlich
  1958   Social Class and Mental Illness: A Community Study. New York:
            Wiley.
Holsti, Ole R.
  1966   "External conflict and internal consensus: The Sino-Soviet case." In
            The General Inquirer, P. J. Stone et al., pp. 342–358. Cambridge:
            M.I.T.
  1969   Content Analysis for the Social Sciences and Humanities. Reading,
            Mass.: Addison-Wesley.
Hong, Lawrence K.
  1984   "List processing free responses: Analysis of open-ended questions
            with word processor." Qualitative Sociology 7:98–109.
Inkeles, Alex
  1973   "Making men modern: On the causes and consequences of individual
            change in six developing countries." In Social Change: Sources, Pat-
            terns, and Consequences. Edited by Amitai Etzioni and Eva Etzioni-
            Halevy, pp. 342–361. 2d ed. New York: Basic Books.
  1983   Exploring Individual Modernity. With contributions by David H.
            Smith and others. New York: Columbia University Press.
Inkeles, Alex, and David H. Smith
  1974   Becoming Modern: Individual Change in Six Developing Countries.
            Cambridge: Harvard University Press.
International Sociological Association
  1955   International Bibliography of Sociology. Volume 5. Prepared by the
            International Committee for Social Sciences Documentation on Co-
            Operation with the International Sociological Association. Paris:
            UNESCO.
Jackson, Mitchell Young
  1939   Minnesota Farmers' Diaries. William R. Brown, 1845–1846; Mitchell
            Young Jackson, 1852–1863. With introduction and notes by Rodney
            C. Loehr. St. Paul: Minnesota Historical Society.
James, William
  1950   The Principles of Psychology. Volume 1. New York: Dover.
Kahn, Herman, and Anthony J. Wiener
  1967a   "The next thirty-three years: A framework for speculation." In
            Toward the Year 2000: Work in Progress, edited by Daniel Bell, pp.
            73–100. Boston: Beacon.
  1967b   The Year 2000. New York: Macmillan.
Kalberg, Stephen
  1980   "Max Weber's types of rationality: Cornerstones for the analysis of
            rationalization processes in history." American Journal of Sociology
            85:1145–1179.
Kasson, John F.
  1976   Civilizing the Machine: Technology and Republican Values in Amer-
            ica 1776–1900. Baltimore: Penguin Books.

Kavolis, Vytautas
1970   "Post-modern man: Psychocultural responses to social trends." Social
        Problems 17:435–448.
Kelly, Edward F., and Phillip J. Stone
1975   Computer Recognition of English Word Senses. Amsterdam: North-
        Holland.
Keniston, Kenneth
1965   The Uncommitted: Alienated Youth in American Society. New York:
        Dell/Laurel.
1968   "The psychology of alienated students." In The Self in Social Inter-
        action, edited by Chad Gordon and Kenneth Gergen, pp. 405–414.
        Volume 1. New York: Wiley.
Kilgore, Dan E.
1978   "How Did Davy Die?" College Station: Texas A&M University Press.
Kogan, David S.
1955   The Diary of David S. Kogan. Edited with introduction by Meyer
        Levin. New York: The Beechurst Press.
Krippendorf, Klaus
1980   Content Analysis: An Introduction to Its Methodology. Beverly Hills:
        Sage.
Kucera, Henry, and W. Nelson Francis
1967   Computational Analysis of Present-Day American English. Provi-
        dence, R.I.: Brown University Press.
Kuhn, Manford H., and Thomas S. McPartland
1954   "An empirical investigation of self-attitudes." American Sociological
        Review 19:68–76.
Kuklick, Bruce
1972   "Myth and symbol in American studies." American Quarterly 24:435–
        450.
Laffal, Julius
1960   "The contextual associates of sun and God in Schreber's autobiog-
        raphy." Journal of Abnormal and Social Psychology 64:474–479.
1965   Pathological and Normal Language. New York: Atherton Press.
1969   "Contextual similarities as a basis for inference." In The Analysis of
        Communication Content, edited by G. Gerbner et al., pp. 159–174.
        New York: Wiley.
1973   A Concept Dictionary of English. Essex, Conn.: Gallery Press.
Landes, David S.
1969   The Unbound Prometheus: Technological Change and Industrial De-
        velopment in Western Europe from 1750 to the Present. Cambridge,
        England: Cambridge University Press.
Lasch, Christopher
1979   The Culture of Narcissism. New York: Norton.
1984   The Minimal Self: Psychic Survival in Troubled Times. New York:
        Norton.
Latham, Robert, and William Matthews (eds.)
1970   The Diary of Samuel Pepys, A New and Complete Transcription.

Volumes 1–11. Berkeley and Los Angeles: University of California Press.

Lawrence, Amos
1855   Extracts from the Diary and a Brief Account of Some Incidents in His Life. Edited by William R. Lawrence, M.D. Boston: Gould and Lincoln.

Lawrence, Ken
1974   "Oral history of slavery." Southern Exposure 1 (3/4):84–86.

Lawrence, Mary Chipman
1966   The Captain's Best Mate: The Journal of Mary Chipman Lawrence on the Whaler Addison 1856–1860. Edited by Stanton Gainer. Providence, R.I.: Brown University Press.

Leary, Louis
1954   Articles on American Literature 1900–1950. Durham: Duke University Press.

Leary, Timothy
1968   The Politics of Ecstasy. New York: Putnam.

Leinberger, Paul
1986   "The 'Organization Man' revisited." New York Times Magazine, Dec. 7, 1986.

Lifton, Robert Jay
1968   "Protean man." Partisan Review 35:13–27.
1969   Boundaries: Psychological Man in Revolution. New York: Simon and Schuster/Touchstone.

Lilienthal, David E.
1964   The Journals of David E. Lilienthal. Volume 1, The TVA Years 1939–1945. Including a Selection of Journal Entries from the 1917–1939 Period. Introduction by Henry Steele Commager. New York: Harper and Row.

Lindbergh, Anne Morrow
1974   Locked Rooms and Open Doors. Diaries and Letters of Anne Morrow Lindbergh 1933–1935. New York: Harcourt, Brace, Jovanovich.

Lindbergh, Charles A.
1970   The Wartime Journals of Charles A. Lindbergh. New York: Harcourt, Brace, Jovanovich.

Lynd, Helen Merrell
1968   "Shame, guilt, and identity beyond roles." In The Self in Social Interaction, edited by Chad Gordon and Kenneth J. Gergen, pp. 219–226. Volume 1. New York: Wiley.

MacFarlane, Alan
1970   The Family Life of Ralph Josselin, A Seventeenth Century Clergyman: An Essay in Historical Anthropology. Cambridge, England: Cambridge University Press.

MacPike, E. F. (comp.)
1944–45   "American and Canadian diaries, journals, and notebooks: Short list." Bulletin of Bibliography 18:91–92, 107–115, 133–135, 156–158.

Madge, John
1962   The Origins of Scientific Sociology. New York: Free Press.

1965   The Tools of Social Science. Garden City, N.Y.: Doubleday/Anchor.

Mariampolski, Hyman, and Dana C. Hughes
1978   "The use of personal documents in historical sociology." American Sociologist 13:104–113.

Markoff, John, Gilbert Shapiro, and Sasha R. Weitman
1974   "Toward the integration of content analysis and general methodology." In Sociological Methodology 1975, edited by David R. Heise, pp. 1–58. San Francisco: Jossey-Bass.

Marx, Karl
1967   Capital: A Critique of Political Economy. Volume 1. The Process of Capitalist Production. Edited by Frederick Engels. New York: International Publishers.

Maslow, Abraham H.
1962   Toward a Psychology of Being. Princeton: D. Van Nostrand.
1969   "Existential psychology—what's in it for us?" In Existential Psychology, edited by Rollo May, pp. 49–57. 2d ed. New York: Random House.

Matthews, William (comp.)
1950   British Diaries: An Annotated Bibliography of British Diaries Written Between 1442 and 1942. Berkeley and Los Angeles: University of California Press.
1959   American Diaries: An Annotated Bibliography of American Diaries Written Prior to the Year 1861. With the assistance of Roy Harvey Pearce. Boston: J. S. Canner.
1974   American Diaries in Manuscript 1580–1954: A Descriptive Bibliography. Athens: University of Georgia Press.

McLaughlin, Barry
1966   "The WAI dictionary and self-perceived identity in college students." In The General Inquirer, P. J. Stone et al., pp. 546–548. Cambridge: M.I.T.

Mead, George Herbert
1934   Mind, Self, and Society: From the Standpoint of a Social Behaviorist. Edited with introduction by Charles W. Morris. Chicago: University of Chicago Press.

Merton, Robert K.
1968   Social Theory and Social Structure. Enl. ed. Glencoe: Free Press.

Miller, Delbert C.
1977   Handbook of Research Design and Social Measurement. 3d ed. New York: David McKay.

Miller, Douglas T.
1970   The Birth of Modern America 1820–1850. Indianapolis: Bobbs-Merrill.

Modern Humanities Research Association
1921   Annual Bibliography of English Language and Literature. Volume 1. Cambridge, England: Bowes and Bowes.

Moffat, Mary Jane, and Charlotte Painter (eds.)
1974   Revelations: Diaries of Women. New York: Random House/Vintage.

Moran, Benjamin
1948   The Journal of Benjamin Moran. Volume 1. 1857–1865 Edited by Sarah

Agnes Wallace and Frances Elma Gilespie. Chicago: University of Chicago Press.

Morse, Abner
  1939–40 "The Abner Morse diary: River Falls, 1859–61." Edited with introduction by Bayard Still and William Herrmann. Wisconsin Magazine of History XXIII:62–88.

Motte, Jacob Rhett
  1940   Charleston Goes to Harvard: The Diary of a Harvard Student of 1831. Edited by Arthur H. Cole. Cambridge: Harvard University Press.

Namenwirth, J. Zvi, and Thomas L. Brewer
  1966   "Elite editorial comment in the European and Atlantic communities in four countries." In The General Inquirer, P. J. Stone et al., pp. 401–427. Cambridge: M.I.T.

Nicholsen, Margaret E.
  1969   People in Books: A Guide to Bibliographical Literature Arranged by Vocations and Other Fields of Reader Interest. New York: H. W. Wilson.

Nie, Norman H., C. Hadlai Hull, Jean G. Jenkins, Karin Steinbrenner, and Dale H. Bent
  1975   SPSS: Statistical Package for the Social Sciences. 2d ed. New York: McGraw-Hill.

Nilon, Charles H.
  1970   Bibliography of Bibliographies in American Literature. New York and London: R. R. Bowker.

Ogilvie, Daniel M., Philip J. Stone, and Edwin S. Shneidman
  1966   "Some characteristics of genuine versus simulated suicide notes." In The General Inquirer, P. J. Stone et al., pp. 527–535. Cambridge: M.I.T.

Ogilvie, Daniel M., Philip J. Stone, and Edward F. Kelly
  1980   "Computer-aided content analysis." In Qualitative Methods. Handbook of Social Science Methods. Edited by Robert B. Smith and Peter K. Manning, pp. 219–246. Volume 2. Cambridge: Ballinger.

Paige, Jeffrey M.
  1966   "Letters from Jenny: An approach to the clinical analysis of personality structure by computer." In The General Inquirer, P. J. Stone et al., pp. 431–451. Cambridge: M.I.T.

Park, Robert E., and Herbert A. Miller
  1921   Old World Traits Transplanted. New York: Harper.

Parsons, Talcott
  1968   The Structure of Social Action: A Study in Social Theory With Special Reference to a Group of Recent European Writers. Volume 2. New York: The Free Press.

Parsons, Talcott, and Edward A. Shills, with James Olds
  1951   "Values, motives, and systems of action." In Toward a General Theory of Action, T. Parsons and E. A. Shills, eds., pp. 47–243. Cambridge: Harvard University Press.

Patterson, Giles
  1944   Journal of a Southern Student 1846–1848. With Letters of a Later

Period. Biographical note by Henry Nelson Snyder. Edited with introduction by Richard Croom Beatty. Nashville: Vanderbilt University Press.

Plummer, Ken
1983   Documents of Life: An Introduction to the Problems and Literature of a Humanistic Method. London: Allen and Unwin.

Ponsonby, Arthur
1923   English Diaries: A Review of English Diaries from the Sixteenth to the Twentieth Century with an Introduction on Diary Writing. London: Methuen.

Pool, Ithiel de Sola
1959   "Trends in content analysis today: A summary." In Trends in Content Analysis, edited by I. de S. Pool, pp. 189–233. Urbana: University of Illinois Press.

Pool, Ithiel de Sola et al.
1970   The Prestige Press: A Comparative Study of Political Symbols. Cambridge: M.I.T.

Prince, Hezekiah
1975   Journals of Hezekiah Prince, Jr. 1822–1828. Introduction by Walter Muir Whitehill. New York: Crown/Maine Historical Society.

Progoff, Ira
1975   At a Journal Workshop: The Basic Text and Guide for Using the Intensive Journal Process. New York: Dialogue House Library.

The Publisher's Trade List Annual
1957   Subject Guide to Books in Print: An Index to the Publishers Trade. New York: R. R. Bowker.

Rainer, Tristine
1978   The New Diary: How to Use a Journal for Self-Guidance and Expanded Creativity. Los Angeles: J. P. Tarcher.

Reich, Charles A.
1970   The Greening of America. New York: Bantam Books.

Rieff, Philip
1966   The Triumph of the Therapeutic: Uses of Faith after Freud. New York: Harper and Row.

Riesman, David
1961   The Lonely Crowd: A Study of the Changing American Character. With Nathan Glazer and Reuel Denney. Abridged Edition. New Haven: Yale University Press.

Rogers, Carl R.
1969   "Toward a modern approach to values: The valuing process in the mature person." In Theory and Research in Abnormal Personality, edited by David Rosenhan and Perry London, pp. 211–22. New York: Holt, Rinehart and Winston.

1972   "A humanistic conception of man." In Humanistic Society: Today's Challenge to Sociology, edited by John F. Glass and John R. Staude, pp. 19–32. Pacific Palisades, Calif.: Goodyear.

Roszak, Theodore
1969   The Making of a Counter Culture: Reflections on the Technocratic

Society and Its Youthful Opposition. Garden City, N.Y.: Doubleday/ Anchor.

Rubin, Theodore Isaac, M.D.
1972   Emergency Room Diary. New York: Grosset and Dunlap.

Rudner, Richard S.
1966   Philosophy of Social Science. Englewood Cliffs, N.J.: Prentice-Hall.

Sanders, Tobi Gillian
1970   Members of the Class Will Keep Daily Journals: The Barnard College Journals of Tobi Gillian Sanders and Joan Frances Bennett, Spring 1968. New York: Winter House.

Schluchter, Wolfgang
1981   The Rise of Western Rationalism: Max Weber's Developmental History. Translated with introduction by Guenter Roth. Berkeley: University of California Press.

Schneider, Louis
1971   "Dialectic in sociology." American Sociological Review 36:667–678.

Schneider, Louis, and Louis A. Zurcher, Jr.
1970   "Toward understanding the Catholic crisis: Observations on dissident priests in Texas." Journal for the Scientific Study of Religion 9:197–209.

Schneider, Louis, and S.M. Dornbusch
1958   Popular Religion: Inspirational Books in America. Chicago: University of Chicago Press.

Schreber, Daniel Paul
1955   Memoirs of My Nervous Illness. Translated and edited, with introduction, notes and discussion by Ida Macalpine and Richard A. Hunter. London: William Dawson and Sons.

Seidel, John V., and Jack A. Clark
1984   "The ETHNOGRAPH: A computer program for the analysis of qualitative data." Qualitative Sociology 7:110–125.

Shaw, Clifford H.
1930   The Jack Roller: A Delinquent Boy's Own Story. Chicago: University of Chicago Press.

Sheehy, Eugene P. (comp.)
1976   Guide to Reference Books. 9th ed. With the assistance of Rita G. Keckeissen and Eileen McIlvane. Chicago: American Library Association.

Sheinberg, Shelia
1974   "Alienated Youth—Fact or Artifact?: Anomy, and Self-Referrent Constructs as 'Pivotal' Variables in a Study of Academic Youth." Ph.D. dissertation, University of Houston.

Shils, Edward
1965   "Charisma, order and status." American Sociological Review 30:199–213.

Simmel, Georg
1971   Georg Simmel on Individuality and Social Forms: Selected Writings. Edited with introduction by Donald N. Levine. Chicago: University of Chicago Press.

Singelmann, Joachim
    1978   From Agriculture to Services: The Transformation of Industrial Employment. Beverly Hills: Sage.
Slater, Philip E.
    1970   The Pursuit of Loneliness: American Culture at the Breaking Point. Boston: Beacon.
Smith, Marshall S., Philip J. Stone, and Evelyn N. Glenn
    1966   "A content analysis of twenty presidential nomination acceptance speeches." In The General Inquirer, P. J. Stone et al., pp. 359–400. Cambridge: M.I.T.
Smith, Sidonie
    1974   Where I'm Bound: Patterns of Slavery and Freedom in Black American Autobiography. Westport, Conn.: Greenwood Press.
Snow, David A., and Cynthia L. Phillips
    1982   "The changing self-orientations of college students: From institution to impulse." Social Science Quarterly 63:462–476.
Sorokin, Pitirim
    1957   Social and Cultural Dynamics: A Study of Change in Major Systems of Art, Truth, Ethics, Law and Social Relationships. Revised and abridged in one volume by the author. Boston: Porter Sargent.
Sorrentino, Constance
    1971   "Comparing employment shifts in 10 industrialized countries." Monthly Labor Review 94:3–11.
Spengemann, William C., and L. R. Lundquist
    1965   "Autobiography and the American myth." American Quarterly 17:501–519.
Spiller, Robert Ernest (ed.)
    1974   Literary History of the United States. 4th ed., rev. New York: Macmillan.
Spitzer, Stephan P., and Jerry Parker
    1976   "Perceived validity and assessment of the self." Sociological Quarterly 17:236–246.
Spitzer, Stephan, Carl Couch, and John Stratton
    1973   The Assessment of the Self. Iowa City: Sernoll.
Stanback, Thomas M., Jr., Peter J. Bearse, Thierry J. Noyelle, and Robert A. Karasek
    1981   Services: The New Economy. Totowa, N.J.: Allanheld, Osmun and Co.
Stone, Albert E.
    1972   "Autobiography and American culture." American Studies 11:22–36.
Stone, Philip J., Dexter C. Dunphy, Marshall S. Smith, Daniel M. Ogilvie, and Associates
    1966   The General Inquirer: A Computer Approach to Content Analysis. Cambridge: M.I.T.
Strachey, James
    1962   "Sigmund Freud: A sketch of his life and ideas." In On the History of the Psycho-Analytic Movement, Sigmund Freud, pp. vii-xvii.

Translation by Joan Riviere. Revised and edited by James Strachey. New York: Norton.   ·

Szczepanski, Jan

1965   "Die biographische methode." *In* Handbuch der Empirischen Sozialforschung. Vol. I. Pp. 551–569. Edited by Rene Konig. Stuttgart: Enke.

1981   "The use of autobiographies in historical social psychology." *In* Biography and Society, edited by Daniel Bertaux, pp. 225–234. Beverly Hills: Sage.

Thayer, H. S.

1968   Meaning and Action: A Critical History of Pragmatism. Indianapolis: Bobbs-Merrill.

Thomas, W. I., and Florian Znaniecki

1958   The Polish Peasant in Europe and America. New York: Dover.

Thrasher, Frederick M.

1927   The Gang. Chicago: University of Chicago Press.

Toennies, Ferdinand

1957   Community and Society (Gemeinschaft and Gesellschaft). Translated and edited by Charles P. Loomis. New York: Harper and Row/Harper Torchbooks.

Toffler, Alvin

1970   Future Shock. New York: Random House.

1980   The Third Wave. New York: Morrow.

Trilling, Lionel

1972   Sincerity and Authenticity. Cambridge: Harvard University Press.

Turner, Ralph

1976   "The real self: From institution to impulse." American Journal of Sociology 81:989–1016.

Turner, Ralph, and Jerald Schutte

1981   "The true self method for studying the self-conception." Symbolic Interaction 4:1–20.

U.S. Library of Congress

1960   A Guide to the Study of the United States of America: Representative Books Reflecting the Development of American Life and Thought. Prepared under the direction of Roy P. Basler by Donald H. Mugridge and Blanche P. McCrum. Washington, D.C.: U.S. Government Printing Office.

1968   The National Union Catalog, Pre–1956 Imprints: A Cumulative Author List Representing Library of Congress Printed Cards and Titles Reported by Other American Libraries. Compiled and edited with the cooperation of the Library of Congress and the National Union Subcommittee of the Resources Committee of the Resource and Technical Services Division, American Library Association. London: Mansell.

Viewegh, J.

1972   K Uziti Osobnich Dokumentu V Psychologii ("The use of personal documents in psychology"). Ceskoslovenska Psychologie 16:363–372.

Walker, Don D.
1974   "The mountain man journal: Its significance in a literary history of the fur trade." Western Historical Quarterly 5:307–318.
Weber, Max
1927   General Economic History. Translated by Frank H. Knight. Glencoe: Free Press.
1946   From Max Weber: Essays in Sociology. Translated and edited, with introduction by H. H. Gerth and C. Wright Mills. New York: Oxford University Press.
1958   The Protestant Ethic and the Spirit of Capitalism. Translated by Talcott Parsons. With foreword by R. H. Tawney. New York: Charles Scribner's Sons.
1968   Max Weber on Charisma and Institution Building: Selected Papers. Edited with introduction by S. N. Eisenstadt. Chicago: University of Chicago Press.
1978a   Economy and Society. Edited by Guenther Roth and Claus Wittich. Berkeley: University of California Press.
1978b   Max Weber: Selections in Translation. Edited by W. G. Runciman. Translated by E. Matthews. Cambridge, England: Cambridge University Press.
Weber, Robert Philip
1983   "Measurement models for content analysis." Quality and Quantity 17:127–149.
1984   "Computer-aided content analysis: A short primer." Qualitative Sociology 7:126–147.
1985   Basic Content Analysis. Beverly Hills: Sage.
Weisberger, Bernard A.
1969   The New Industrial Society. New York: Wiley.
Wheaton, Ellen Birdseye
1923   The Diary of Ellen Birdseye Wheaton. With notes by Donald Gordon. Boston: Privately printed (D. B. Updike, Merrymount Press).
Whyte, Willam H., Jr.
1957   The Organization Man. Garden City, N.Y.: Doubleday/Anchor.
1986   "The organization man: A rejoinder." New York Times Magazine, Dec. 7, 1986.
Wiener, Norbert
1954   The Human Use of Human Beings: Cybernetics and Society. 2d ed., rev. Garden City, N.Y.: Doubleday/Anchor.
Williams, Frederick
1982   The Communications Revolution. Beverly Hills: Sage.
Wilson, H. W.
1937–42 Bibliographic Index: A Cumulative Bibliography of Bibliographies. Volume 1. New York: H. W. Wilson.
Wood, Michael
1978   "The Postmodern Self: An Analysis of Selected Nineteenth and Twentieth Century American Published Diaries." Unpublished doctoral dissertation. Austin: The University of Texas.

1980   "Alternatives and options in computer content analysis." Social Science Research 9:273–286.

1984   "Using Key-Word-In-Context concordance programs for qualitative and quantitative social research." The Journal of Applied Behavioral Science 20:289–297.

Woodrum, Eric

1984   "'Mainstreaming' content analysis in social science: Methodological advantages, obstacles, and solutions." Social Science Research 13:1–19.

Wrigley, E. A.

1969   Population and History. World University Library. New York: McGraw-Hill.

Yankelovich, Daniel

1981   New Rules: Searching for Self-fulfillment in a World Turned Upside Down. New York: Random House.

Yin, Robert K.

1984   Case Study Research: Design and Methods. Beverly Hills: Sage.

Zimmerman, Don H., and D. Lawrence Wieder

1977   "The diary: Diary-interview method." Urban Life 5:479–498.

Zorbaugh, Harvey W.

1929   The Gold Coast and the Slum. Chicago: University of Chicago Press.

Zurcher, Louis A., Jr.

1967   "Functional marginality: Dynamics of a poverty intervention organization." Social Science Quarterly 48:411–421.

1972a   "The mutable self: An adaptation to accelerated socio-cultural change." et al. 3:3–15.

1972b   "The poor and the hip: Some manifestations of cultural lead." Social Science Quarterly 53:357–387.

1973   "The mutable self and alternative institutions." Journal of Applied Behavioral Science 9:369–380.

1977   The Mutable Self: A Self-Concept for Social Change. Foreword by Ralph Turner. Beverly Hills: Sage.

1986   "The bureaucratizing of impulse: Self-conception in the 1980s." Symbolic Interaction 9:169–178

Index

About the Authors

MICHAEL R. WOOD is Assistant Professor of Sociology at Hunter College of the City University of New York, where he also serves as an instructor in the Graduate Program in Social Research. He has published articles in *American Sociological Review, American Sociologist, Developments in Marketing Science, The Journal of Applied Behavioral Science*, and *Social Science Research*, as well as other social science journals.

LOUIS A. ZURCHER, JR., was Ashbel Smith Distinguished Professor of Social Work and Sociology at the University of Texas, Austin. Among his books were *The Mutable Self* and *Social Roles*; he was co-editor of *Citizen Sailors in a Changing Society: Policy Issues for Manning the United States Naval Reserve* (Greenwood Press, 1986). He was President of the Society for the Study of Symbolic Interaction and Editor of *The Journal of Applied Behavioral Science*.